THE TAO OF RAVEN

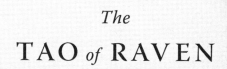

The

TAO *of* RAVEN

AN ALASKA NATIVE MEMOIR

Ernestine Hayes

UNIVERSITY OF
WASHINGTON PRESS
Seattle & London

© 2017 by Ernestine Hayes
First paperback edition 2019
Printed and bound in the United States of America
Jacket and frontis art: Crystal Worl
Design: Dustin Kilgore
Typeset in Warnock, a typeface designed by Robert Slimbach
23   22   21   20   19   5   4   3   2   1

Portions of this work have appeared in similar form in
*Studies in American Indian Literature, Made of Salmon,
Huffington Post, Tidal Echoes, Mud City Journal*, and *49 Writers*.

UNIVERSITY OF WASHINGTON PRESS
www.washington.edu/uwpress

Library of Congress Cataloging-in-Publication Data

Names: Hayes, Ernestine, 1945– author.
Title: The tao of raven : an Alaska native memoir / Ernestine Hayes.
Description: Seattle : University of Washington Press, 2016.
Identifiers: LCCN 2016007836 | ISBN 9780295999593 (hardcover : alk. paper)
Subjects: LCSH: Hayes, Ernestine, 1945– | Tlingit Indians—Alaska—
    Biography. | Tlingit women—Alaska—Biography. | Women college
    teachers—Alaska—Biography. | Homecoming—Alaska. | Tlingit
    Indians—Alaska—Social life and customs. | Tlingit Indians—Alaska—
    Social conditions. | Alaska—Social conditions.
Classification: LCC E99.T6 H39 2016 | DDC 979.8004/9727—dc23
LC record available at https://lccn.loc.gov/2016007836

The paper used in this publication is acid-free and meets
the minimum requirements of American National Standard
for Information Sciences—Permanence of Paper for
Printed Library Materials, ANSI Z39.48–1984. ∞

*For all those who came before me
and all those who come after me*

CONTENTS

At a time so long ago it can be measured neither by following the moon's slow dance nor by tracing the sun's brightened path, had moon and sun then been part of life, darkness was upon the face of the world. This circumstance made it difficult for human beings to conduct their ordinary lives. For example, how much more difficult to impress one another when decisions are made in the dark. How much more difficult to recognize an ally, how much more difficult to praise another's significance, thereby increasing one's own importance. How much more difficult to confront a shadow, to challenge the gloom. In an unbrightened world, light does not reveal itself. It must be stolen.

Liberated. Reclaimed, some might say.

Raven has always and not always been around to be amused at the pitiful antics of self-important human beings, and no doubt he found amusement in the ill-composed conditions of a darkened world. But, although he may have discerned intrigue and opportunity, although he may have sensed illicit adventure, although he could well have been distracted by wonders that he alone could see, nevertheless Raven decided to do something about the darkness.

Raven knew about an old man who lived with his daughter in a well-fortified house in an isolated place at the top of a river far away. This old man, it was said, kept in his house precious bentwood boxes in which could be found answers to the darkness. It was said that this old man guarded these boxes even more carefully than he guarded his daughter. He allowed his daughter to venture outside the house for such purposes as gathering roots and collecting water, but never did he allow his precious boxes to be removed from his house or even to be opened, or even to be looked upon, or even to be named.

Raven decided that it was a good time to investigate. But when Raven traveled to that old man's house, built so close to the Nass River, he was unable to discover an easy entry. In other words, there was no doorway through which he could be invited; there was no window through which he could climb. Though Raven walked around and around and around that old man's house, he never was able to find a direct way to get inside.

But Raven noticed that every once in a while that old man's daughter appeared outside the house and carried a container down to the rippling water, where she filled the woven water-basket from the fresh clear stream. Although Raven studied her every move, he was unable to perceive how she gained entry back into the house.

These riddles kept him puzzling for what would have been days had there been daylight and for what would have been nights had there been stars. After much deliberation, after careful calculation, after he finally decided that the proper moment had arrived, Raven transformed himself into a pine needle and dropped himself into the water that the old man's daughter was about to drink, at which time that old man's daughter, no doubt tasting water sweeter than she had tasted ever before, swallowed Raven in his pine-needle form. When that immediate inevitable moment revealed itself in its endless existence, Raven transformed himself and was transformed and that old man's daughter became pregnant with Raven-child.

After waiting a while inside his mother's womb, Raven allowed himself to be born, whereupon he entered the guarded house and reentered the unguarded world in the manifestation of a newborn human baby. At once he became something more dear to that old man's eyes than even those precious boxes of light.

That delighted grandfather, that old man, loved to pretend to chase his grandchild from the front of his house to the back, past the curtained sleeping crannies, past the piled-high plain wooden boxes of dryfish and seaweed, past the woven water-baskets, past the house posts, past the screen, around again to the opposite wall, catching him and spinning dreams and hopes into the contented air. The old man delighted more and more in his Raven grandchild, playing peek-a-boo games and singing him lullabies and feeding him tender tidbits of salmon cheeks and the steamed soft eggs of seabirds still crying for their young. At the rare times that Raven fussed, the old grandfather bounced baby Raven on his knee and nuzzled baby Raven's neck and checked the moss around baby Raven's sleeping place to satisfy himself that it remained dry and soft and safe.

After a while, after a not-yet-measured time, Raven began to cry for those bentwood boxes. No matter how strong the spirits that protected the boxes and the priceless objects inside, Raven must have been confident that the love his grandparent held for him was deeper and more secure.

When baby Raven cried for the first bentwood box, the old man must surely have thought to refuse. But Raven kept crying, and the old man gave in, just as Raven knew he would do. Raven's grandfather watched him open that first box and admire all the stars that it contained. After only a while, not long enough for a grandparent to feel sated by his grandchild's laugh, Raven tossed the stars into the sky, whereupon our world became brighter by the measure of one Box of Starlight, and the old man's house became darker in the same regard.

Raven cried for the next bentwood box. As Raven knew his grandfather would do, the old man again said no, and when Raven kept crying, the old man finally gave in, just as Raven knew he would do. Raven's grandfather watched him open the second precious box, this one containing the moon. Raven admired the moon for just a little while, perhaps playing with the full moon and again with the waning, and then he tossed the moon into the sky, whereupon our world became brighter by the measure of one Box of Moonlight, and the old man's house became darker in the same regard.

Raven now cried for the last bentwood box. As Raven thought he would do, that old man resisted more than all the other times. And when Raven kept crying, the old man gave in, just as Raven knew that his grandparent would do. And so it was that Raven's grandfather watched him open the last precious box, and Raven struggled light through the smokehole into a newly lighted world, whereupon our human world became brighter by the measure of a Box of Daylight, and the old man's house became dark.

THE TAO OF RAVEN

ONE

Brown Bear Spins beneath the Darkly Spinning Stars

GOALS, LIKE CONSEQUENCES, are ephemeral shades that for those careless/carefree/care-ridden souls grown from generations of the fallen are not— cannot be—related to the natural order. Maybe-someday musings, maybe-it-won't-happen hopes: on such placid determination at the age of fifty, I rested the newly forming image of myself as a woman who could get things done, and I jumped through all the tribal and academic and state and federal hoops into a college classroom full of eighteen-year-olds, where I convinced myself I could remain as I felt I had been all my life. Anonymous. Unnoticed. Unseen.

I sometimes wonder if I would have been able to share my small victories with my mother had she lived long enough to see me go to college, to see me hold down a job, to see me buy a comfortable, warm house. She had been so used to my failures. My failings. She had been so used to my superficial needs, all the needs she thought could be quieted by a five dollar bill, a carton of cigarettes, a twenty-five dollar savings bond cashed as soon as she turned her back or looked the other way. All my infrequent attempts to talk to her—about grappled problems, ungrappled men, stillborn plans—were met with her bewilderment and silence. Changing the channel to a basketball game. Broadcasting another belch and pouring herself another cup of instant coffee: black, bitter, and not quite hot enough to savor. Preparing for the coming day when our unspoken conversations would be about her death. Preparing for her seventy-pound, skeletal frame and her regression to the helpless infanthood that had far too soon been stolen from her. Preparing for her still-unspoken supplications: Carry me. Feed me. Change my linens change my clothes change my future change my past. Change my life. Change me.

Some months after we made it back home to Juneau, my mother began to invite our little family to join her, every year, for Easter brunch at the Baranof Hotel. Just a short walk up the hill from the downtown senior housing apartment where, having outlasted two other tenants, my mother had at last won a coveted corner apartment, the Baranof had long been an emblem of the plush-carpeted luxury normally available only to visiting dignitaries and their guests. On Easter Sundays, though, a grand brunch was open to the paying community. She saved up all year and insisted that the whole family accompany her to the mid-morning holiday meal. Surrounded by her only daughter, her grandsons and their partners, and her great-grandchildren, she persevered step by step up the steep block, her generations ready to support her, ready to catch her should she fall. Finally at the entrance, she could not pull open the thick-windowed brass door, which must have weighed more than she did those last few years of her scarred life. Once inside, she gathered her fearless bluster and strode on skinny stick-legs to the reservations podium, where she claimed our table and welcomed us to the feast, while she picked at salted ham and cream-puffed pastries and fidgeted for her next cigarette, which, after a life spent inhaling the smoke of unfiltered Pall Malls, would eventually, inevitably, predictably, to her utmost surprise, kill her.

For as long as I can remember or Kodak pictures can commemorate, my mother brandished a perpetual frown. When she was growing up she must have lived in constant fear of almost everything in our old family home in the village, almost everything in unfriendly white-man schools and in forbidding white-man churches, almost everything in dark unwelcoming movie theaters, almost everything that came walking toward her down the street or crossed to the other side to avoid her. I imagine that before she was five years old by white-man count, my mother developed the mean scowl that, over the coming years, would quiet fussing baby brothers, whining little sisters, prim-hard teachers, unwary schoolchildren in her grade and on the streets, all the pastors, caseworkers, cannery bosses, secretaries, judges, doctors, every single waiter and every maître d'. I can suppose that she was still afraid of them, but when others were subdued by her frowning facade, she built up the nerve to walk by their widened eyes and find a place to sit with her back against a steady wall and glare everyone else at the Easter banquet into disconcerted silence, while her loving family helped themselves to poached eggs and fresh-cut cubes of melon.

That last year, the year she died, she couldn't take us to the Baranof. She died the day after Easter. By then her concerns no longer centered on seeing us seated at a table that featured real cloth napkins and our choice of fruit juice or champagne. By then, she had abandoned all thought of Pall Mall cigarettes in favor of the loud humming machine that she told herself would help her regrow the lung tissue that emphysema had shriveled, would help her regain the weight and muscle that had vanished breath by ever-shorter breath, would unswell her congested limbs, all that ruined wreckage having now left only her beautiful, textured brown skin covering her still-fierce bones.

Later in the year that she died, I began to jump through the paperwork hoops by which I would ready myself to enroll at the local college.

Free education for Native people is not free. Nor is free health care. Free housing. Free food. In the earlier years of colonization, the Bureau of Indian Affairs crafted its design of educating Indigenous people for service to the master, which would require at most the completion of a two-year program, perhaps in carpentry, perhaps in clerical support, perhaps in cooking, cleaning, filing. Through the decades, those archaic programs changed only with regard to the number of bureaucratic layers required to shuffle the growing paperwork thrown in front of the would-be student. So it was that I enrolled in the likeliest two-year program offered at the local campus, choosing my classes according to the checkboxes on a form that promised an associate's degree at the end of four semesters.

Thus began my formal exploration of the master's written word. Laboring in the garden of the master's ivory tower, as it were, although in the coming years I learned that the path from the master's porch to the master's parlor was not an easy one for the likes of me. On those occasions when I was allowed a peek into the Europhile parlor, it was clear to me that I would rather walk barefoot through the master's garden on my way to the raindark forest where the master never trod than sit in an ivory parlor sipping imported tea from dainty cups embossed with gilt-ridden letters that proclaimed the bearer's legitimacy. Much like old stories told of unsuspecting Native people carrying letters to demonstrate their integrity to white traders: The Bearer of this Letter, the ivory tower missive might read, is a Low-Down Scoundrel Convinced that Institutional Recognition Renders Him More Qualified Than Everybody Else.

The intended joke, of course, is that in his simplicity, the ingenuous Native trader cannot understand that another culture has different standards, different values, different priorities that render the piece of paper upon which he believes his credentials rest no more than that: a piece of paper proclaiming virtues that can be demonstrated only by one's behavior. But a trickster is always at work: that revered piece of paper is the ticket not to the master's table but into the master's banquet hall, where careless crumbs brushed from the master's gilded plate can be reclaimed and fashioned into rotting compost to nourish the forest floor.

We spend our years as we have done throughout the accumulated decades: we construct elaborate deceptions to steady ourselves against the irresistible onslaught. In the meantime, we entertain ourselves with petty pleasures: How shall we live? How shall our children and grandchildren survive? How are we ever to find our way? Young men comfortable in unknowing privilege and unacknowledged power ask innocent questions and recoil at the raw answer: you have been made god, and you must behold what you have wrought.

Ahh, but there's no good reason to dwell on daily irritations when the glimpse of a world contained in the most delicate drop of iridescent morning stuns us in our uncertain tracks, where the echoed hints of a raven's flight and the eagle's wing pass so close we are able to sense the rush of disturbing wind, where memories of imagined happinesses and constructed deceptions are unceasingly re-created in the music of our temperate rain, splashing on the surface of the constant, gaping ocean.

✤ ‖ ✤

One scrap of earth. No larger than can be made into a cabin comfortable enough for one resolute woman of minor needs and few desires. A modest garden border, to allow sunlight and satisfy curious bears. A few windows, to allow in the day and upon which the morning's rain can be measured. The rich wet smell of cedar, like a mother's tender arms. Her kiss on my hair. The touch of her young hand on my worn cheek. A warm smoky fire. The clatter of the poker against a crumbling log. Outside, a raven's cry.

Do you see the water at the top of the creek, at the top of the mountain that holds our town in the palm of its hand and seeks the shoreline that our own front doors face? Be like that water.

Be yielding like water.

Go along the easiest way always, always willing to go around something. Offer no resistance. Go the easy way. That's the best way to get where you're going. Remember that all things begin and end in water, just as rivers begin and flow into the sea. When forces oppose, victory will be kind to the one who crafts herself like water, to the one whose power allows her to yield.

Take Raven.

When he wanted the Box of Daylight, he didn't invade a village. He didn't storm a house. He found the easy way. He used water. He made himself small so he could get close to daylight with the least effort. This is what Raven did to achieve his goal.

More than ravens cry upon this scrap of tender earth. History cries. Our grandfathers cry. Raven's beloved aunties cry for him. Wolves cry for their namesakes. The bear takes pity when he hears us cry for his protection. The ground is covered with tears.

More than tears cover the ground on this scrap of sodden earth. More than ice. More than glaciers. More than light and dark and shadow. Hemlock and spruce hold hands and gaze at the rainwashed moon. Blueberry bushes call hello to their salmonberry cousins. Wood ferns cluster, devil's club soothes. Mosses ruffle and creep.

Do you hear the movements and calls of life on the fragrant air and in the ready sea and at every place around us? Those calls and tears and cries all signify time. Constantly they remind us that we cannot rush the bloom. Often they tell us we must find a good place to wait.

When making a move will not gain an advantage and your position is already secure, do not move. Place yourself in a defensible position. When it is your choice to hesitate— to wait for a while—do so at an advantageous spot, after all certain progress has been made. When you defend your position, be like one who has held on and pulled herself up to a steep place on a high cliff with a Chilkat mountain at her back, one who has kicked her rope off the ledge and has resolved to engage the battle. From that firm position, make your careful calculations. From that unyielding position, study the circumstances out of which you will assemble victory. From that resolute position, become acquainted with the disposition of your adversary.

Take Raven.

After he had made himself into a pine needle and caused a young woman to swallow him, he stayed in her belly where he could hear and understand all that was taking place around him. From that vantage, he listened and waited for the right moment to make his move. From that position, he studied his circumstances and began to recognize his grandfather's weakness. This is what Raven did to achieve his goal.

⊹ ‖ ⊹

Old Tom walks along the beach. Low tide has set the table. He hopes for clams, urchins, maybe a crab. This part of the beach, a hidden button of a cove that only he knows, has never yielded much in the way of bounty, but on a mild afternoon with a few clouds reflected in the tide pools and amid the thick rich stench of the beach, it makes a fine day. Old Tom builds a fire.

It's been a few years now since Old Tom lost his son, a few years since word came that Young Tom's skiff had been found and no sign of Young Tom. Only his wrinkled campsite, only the ashes of his fire. Only the now empty places that Young

Tom's body once filled, the empty air where his voice once rang, the empty promises Young Tom always meant to keep. Old Tom never thinks about the moment he heard the news without experiencing again the immediate cold dread that erupted from his groin through his belly into his chest and pierced his suddenly sober mind. He'd like to say he never drank again. He'd like to say he drank until the funeral and never drank after that. He'd like to say he sobered up a few weeks or a few months later for the sake of the memory of his son. But he kept drinking until the doctor at the Indian clinic told him it was get sober or die, and after three more benders when getting drunk made him sicker than staying sober and drinking was no longer the way to get well, Old Tom got sober. And now he walks along the beach and thinks of days and nights and laughs and smiles and kisses and women and snow and cold and warm salt water and his son his only son his boy his baby boy Young Tom.

After Young Tom and Lucille split up and Young Tom finally married Mabel, it looked like there would be a family in the family after all. A place where Old Tom could say he could go on holidays like Thanksgiving and Easter. A place to think about when he shivered in an abandoned car on a cold night and crooned lovesongs to the darkness, feeling sorry for himself and missing the one woman in the world who for a while before she died had said she loved him. A place that formed the picture of a granddaughter and a son and a woman named Mabel to hold onto like the thought of white people's heaven to the unsaved.

Old Tom had often gazed at the Fosbee Apartments balanced on the hill above him while he sat in any current version of any broken-down car in a windy freeze or a warm rain, on a morning or a night alone. On those nights when pals stuffed themselves into the car to help him drink, he didn't pay attention to anything outside, let alone the cracked paint peeling from the sides of a building that might once have been new and expensive and fresh but now was no more than a worn reminder of who was meant to lay claim to the top and who was meant to remain at the bottom. Old Tom was just doing his job.

So that day when Young Tom gathered a bunch of the boys out of Pocket Park, across the street from the handiest liquor store and the friendliest bar and said he wanted to take a walk to go and see his daughter, Old Tom was glad to go along. "Sure! I'll go along!" he promised his boy and patted Young Tom on the back of his oily Carhartt jacket, still his pride and pleasure after years of fishing and working and being arrested and partying and sleeping in the thing. He'd probably die in it. "You'll probably die in this jacket, son! You never take it off!" They all laughed.

The seven of them staggered up Franklin Street as far as the Baranof Hotel and cut over to Seward. They found good places to sit on benches near the bear sculpture, taking cover in the early evening shade, hiding from cops in the cemented walkway of the courthouse. "The cops'll never look for us at the courthouse," they laughed, and passed around a couple of bottles, one a green glass bottle of sweet cheap wine and one a see-through pint of sharp cheap vodka.

Everything cheap, but nothing as cheap as the price they were forced to take for all their land and their whole way of life. Nothing so dear as the price paid for uninvited strangers coming in and taking over and teaching them they had to try to be like those white strangers in every way while at the same time every new thing letting them know they could never really be like those white people, not in this life or the next no never not at all. They just had to wait and hope they made it into the white man's heaven and in the meantime they could either try to be white or they could just say hell with it, let's drink.

"Hell with it!" Old Tom laughed. "Let's drink!"

One by one starting with Young Tom they resumed the walk toward the Fosbee. When Young Tom reached the curving corner across from the city museum, Old Tom made up his mind that he'd go all the way with his son. He raised himself up off the cement step butt first, his bad leg not worth trying to stand on, pulling himself up with one hand on the smooth wrought steel handhold, his other hand in the pocket of a thin windbreaker not meant for a man like him in a place like this on an evening in what had become of Alaska, gripping a secret bottle dedicated to taking the edge off his daily hard times. By the time Old Tom shuffled across the street, stopping approaching cars with one shaky hand, Young Tom was already propping himself against the chain-link fence at the top of the stairs where everybody knew the view of the Indian Village below was the only best thing left of their lives. Old Tom pressed on.

Old Tom and Young Tom admired the view and shared sips of secret courage. A couple of ravens scolded them but they paid no mind. A few seagulls circled and took off for the harbor. No eagles today.

"What's my granddaughter doing at the Fosbee Apartments, son?" Old Tom felt like his son had told him, but he couldn't be sure. Best always to know things.

"Some white lady took her when her mom went away." Young Tom pinched snot from his nose. He hoped he wouldn't cry in front of his dad. "I got back from fishing and the place was empty. When I left, Lucille was gone but I thought she'd be back like always." He took another sip of courage. "Guess this time I was wrong again."

Behind them, Isaac inched over the crosswalk, Alfred the Skiff Man right behind him, two cars waiting. The sight of property-owning white people waiting on a drunk Indian made Old Tom take practical measure of the better part of valor. "Let's keep walking then," he warned Young Tom. After one more sip they tore their eyes from the Indian Village below them and headed toward the governor's mansion, where they made a wide left. The Fosbee Apartments appeared at the end of the short street, presenting the next good place to sit while they waited for the rest of the gang to catch up.

In the quiet dusk of a day not easily recalled—where had he been when he woke up this morning?—Old Tom sat beside his son at the top of the metal stairs leading down to Capitol Avenue and polished off the vodka in dainty sips, now and then offering with shaky callused hands the clear liquid treasure to Young Tom for a sip, now and then glancing up the street to check Isaac and Alfred the Skiff Man's progress and behind them the progress of another three people. It looked like one of them had picked up a couple of girls.

"Looks like that one young buck picked up a couple of girls." Old Tom tongued the last trickle from the hollow bottle and tossed it into the thick clumps of devil's club bushes and hemlock trees growing on the hillside. Too much shade here for berries to grow. Old Tom waited for the messy sound of the empty liquor bottle landing on the steep forest floor.

After the prolonged rustle of the bottle's fall, gentled by a few remaining leaves and softened branches, there came the satisfying slap of the thrown bottle striking the other bottles hidden in the undergrowth. Old Tom glanced behind them and then at his son. "There goes another dead soldier, son." They both nodded with the wisdom and knowledge that such a truth could bring. "Must be enough to make an army by now."

Young Tom agreed. "Yep. Enough to make a tribe."

"Enough to build a clan," Old Tom laughed. "It's a good hiding place! We should try to hide in there some time!"

Alfred the Skiff Man shuffled up to stand outside the door of the Fosbee. "I don't know if I can make it down those stairs," he cautioned. "I might have to hold on to somebody if I'm going to try."

"Don't worry about it, friend," Young Tom assured him. "We're going inside the Fosbee to visit my daughter."

"Oh, okay. Good thing."

The other two men walked up, two girls giggling behind them. "We got a party," one of the girls called out.

Young Tom frowned and shushed the girls. "We have to act like we know how to act," he said. "This is a white lady. She's holding onto my daughter."

"Sure! We can do that," they all agreed. "Lead the way."

The girls giggled again. "We'll be right behind you," one of them promised the raggedy men.

Young Tom led the way. He'd been here two or three times already, but so far this Mabel lady hadn't let him in. She always said to come back when he was sober. "She always tells me to come back when I'm sober," he announced to the crowd behind him. "So this time everybody act sober."

They negotiated the short walk down the hall to the right with only a few bumps into the walls and a few more giggles from the girls. At the designated door, Young Tom took a calming breath and readied himself to knock. Glancing back to assess the crowd, he caught Leonard taking a sip. "Hey!" Young Tom stage-whispered. "Hey! What are you doing!"

Leonard tucked the bottle back in the waistband of his jeans. "Nothing," he assured his friend.

"Okay. Let me have a sip then," Young Tom said. "I just need a little bit more courage for when this white woman opens the door this time." He took a gulp and handed it back to Leonard. "All right then," he encouraged himself with a few quick nods and a deep determined sigh. "All right. I can do this."

He raised his fist to knock. The chainlocked door opened a few inches. In the chained space, a mean white-lady frown appeared.

"What do you think you're doing!" the white lady hissed through disapproving pursed lips.

The young buck and two girls retreated backwards down the hall. Leonard backed away a couple of steps. Old Tom hitched his pants and turned toward the exit while everyone else was still negotiating their retreat. Young Tom struggled for words.

Behind the white lady, a little girl's voice called. "Daddy?"

Young Tom's courage rose up again. "I want to see my daughter."

Mabel intensified her frown. "I told you to come back when you are sober, Thomas. If you don't leave immediately, I'm calling the police."

"Young Tom."

"I beg your pardon?"

"Young Tom. My name is Young Tom. Not Thomas. I want to see my daughter. Please."

"Daddy?"

The white lady turned her face. "Patricia, go sit over there, honey. Your father's not in any condition to visit you right now. He can come back when he feels better." She turned back to Young Tom. "I'm closing the door and I'm calling the police." She shut the door.

Young Tom made it to the top of the metal stairs in one or two seconds flat. Everyone else, including Albert the Skiff Man on now-nimble legs, was at least halfway down the stairs on their way to Capitol Avenue. In less than a minute, Young Tom had caught up to his father and they were stepping in the downhill direction of the village. At the edge of the village, Old Tom beelined for a green-striped rattletrap station wagon resting on two flat tires and two bare rims. He pried open the doors. "I still have a little bit of vodka hidden in this one," he announced. Everyone piled in.

Young Tom sat in the front, Old Tom at the wheel. They passed around bottles that appeared from nowhere. They ignored the smell of piss and sour wine. They played with the radio though it made no sound. They listened to the rain on the roof. Above them on the hill, the Fosbee Apartments loomed. Every now and then as darkness crept up from the ground, Young Tom thought he could see his daughter sitting at the window watching them, learning from her father and grandfather the way her family should act, learning from that white lady Mabel the way her family should be treated.

Mabel's own father had hugged her once, on the day they buried Mabel's mother. Mabel was twelve, the second child of six, but the oldest girl. It was already up to her to tend to her four younger sisters and to clean up after the whole family. When her mother had grown sickly, Mabel nursed her as well as she could and added laundry and cooking to her list of chores. When her mother died after seven months of failing health—first a forced reluctant nap on a random afternoon, then early to bed almost every evening, finally spending all day every day in the dark sweaty bed in the dark sweaty room Mabel's father by then refused to enter—Mabel took on more and more responsibilities until it was a final relief when Mabel's mother gave up her submissive ghost and passed on to quiet glory.

She's gone to join the Lord, the neighbors comforted. Here's my special hominy casserole, my favorite snap bean soup, my oxtail jelly broth. How's your father doing, the widows asked. How's your brother, asked the widows' daughters. No one asked how was Mabel, how were her sisters, how were those last bad days with her mother's moaning and pissed sheets and frightened begging eyes filling all of Mabel's days and, worse, all of her nights. At the funeral Mabel got an uneasy hug from her father, a solitary pat on her back, and afterwards back at home, a quick "What's for dinner?" from him, accompanied by oppressive needy stares from her older brother and four younger sisters. In five years she was gone for good, working her way through high school and then business school, never looking back, never visiting, never keeping in touch, never falling in love, never marrying, never having children of her own. She'd moved to Alaska on an adventurous lark to become one of the few single white women in the territory and settled down to a life of tranquil satisfaction, joining a Sunday-only church, keeping her own counsel, minding her own apartment and her own business. She imagined that her father was long dead. She almost never thought about that one hug from her father on the loneliest of days at her mother's plain funeral.

Now things had turned out that Mabel was like a mother to Patricia. No one could say it wasn't true. Lucille, Patricia's real mom, had left town when Patricia was still in grade school. Left town when Patricia was sick. Left her when she asked for some peppermint candy from the store up the street. Left Patricia when her stuffy nose kept her from breathing and she had bitten and pulled the loose skin on her chapped lips until they bled and stung. Left without a sideways glance or feeble goodbye when all Patricia wanted was a sober hug. She asked her mom for some peppermint candy and Lucille said, okay what the hell, gave her sniffling daughter a thin squeeze, and let the uncaring door close itself behind her.

Every time Patricia's dad left home, carrying his gear down to the dock to board whatever boat would hire him, and went off to spend a few days or a week or the whole summer fishing, things got hard and dirty, but Patricia always held to the hope that she would catch from the corner of her itching eye the movement of the doorknob turning, would feel an expectant half-smile forming on her half-healed bitten lips, would hold her mucus-filled breath inside her wheezing chest, and through the door would walk her dad, holding out for her waiting hands a sticky peppermint prize. But when the indifferent door hesitantly sealed the silhouette of a now-gone Lucille in the middle of the one-way threshold, all of Patricia's hopes drained into the rippling gutter with all of tomorrow's hard dirty rains.

◦ ‖ ◦

Summer days in Juneau were sweeter when I was a girl, the breezes more gentle, the sun's rays warmer, the laughter more spontaneous, the possible future imprecise but somehow bright. The distinctions that divided me from other children—wrinkled dirty clothes, absence of family at schooltime celebrations, unclean fingernails and dirty hands, no doubt a salty, unwashed smell—had eased upon my mother's return from her long tubercular stay in the hospital, and the separation from my classmates that would arrive with puberty was still no more than a wistfully approaching shadow. At that in-between age, anyone I met on my summer-day wanderings might become a one-day friend. Anyone might join me for a rambling day of hiking up Mt. Roberts, wading down Gold Creek, fishing off the city dock. So it was that morning that I met two or three classmates, not quite strangers, not at all friends, white kids who lived in neighborhoods I didn't know, who wore clothes that were purchased from places other than the mail-order catalogs my mother and I so eagerly anticipated, who attended churches where their parents—mothers and fathers praying together at elegant polished pews, walking hand in arm from dusted doorstep to reserved parking place, living together in veiled discontent and virtuous disapproval—or was that simply what I'd already learned to tell myself in order to construct solace in an unconsoling world—gave thanks to a just god who had arranged their success and guaranteed their continued rewards and those of their blessed children, in whom they were all so well pleased. After some hellos, we decided to walk over to the docks to try out the new fishing pole one of them had just been given by his father. I promised to take a picture with my mother's Kodak that she had lovingly consigned to me for the summer.

The experience of fishing off the docks was always marred for me by the sight of the struggling gasping creature, eyes bugged, delirious, terrified, bloody hook pulling at its thin lip, fighting with all the might of its soon-to-be succulent flesh for the freedom of the green water lapping the slimy barnacle-covered pilings beneath our feet. My own fishing escapades had mainly been limited to hunting for already-severed halibut heads outside the loud wide doors of the cold storage, which in a year or two would burst into a fire so large it woke the whole town, including my mother, who would walk me by the hand to witness the extraordinary sight of high flames lighting the unstarred darkness.

Our chatter was that of children, the excitement of a nibble now and then neither fulfilled nor defeated by success or by failure. It was enough to be alive. I sensed the possibilities contained in friendship with these extraordinary children, the promise of entry, a relief from freedom, the security of belonging. Along with their friendship might come comfort, might come knowledge, might come understanding. Along with their friendship might come acceptance. I might be included. I might belong.

The blond-haired boy began to snigger. "Look at that drunk Indian carrying that fish. Let's get out of here." He pointed southward down the dock and began to wind in his line. I followed his eyes in the direction of his pointing finger to see an old man in a greasy wool jacket, dark fisherman's knit cap covering his head, a fresh halibut glistening from a length of twine wrapped around his fist.

I squinted. "That's my grandfather," I announced to the boy and his fidgety, giggling companions.

Everyone tried to be quiet as my grandfather walked toward us. The other children, their derision ill-concealed by poor attempts to cover their snorts of laughter, took hesitant steps backward as my grandfather neared. Finally we all stood too close to one another, within the distance of a man's height, his reach, his life, the white children I'd dared to imagine as my friends staging their retreat behind me, ready to dash for the safety of another world, my grandfather in front of me, offering a whiskered smile, saluting me with the heavy flatfish he proudly held up for my regard and admiration, I at the torn seam of two worlds, dreams faded like dappling sunlight, the only choice no choice at all, to embrace the life that had been designed for me no less than the lives that had been designed by these children's parents for us all, to give back the proud smile my grandfather offered, to know that despite the fish slime, despite the days-old whiskers, despite the headache and lost fingers and sharp grief, here was a man who understood what it meant to be proud. I took his picture and gave him a hug. I admired the salt-fresh fish. We both knew he would sell it to some lucky cook and would use the money to buy more wine. We both knew it would take far more than a sunny afternoon for me to make friends of those softened, pink children. We both knew that those children's fathers, though they ran the town and ran the schools and ran the courts and ran our lives, would never possess the courage that my grandfather showed every day by simply waking up and going on. We both knew that even though halibut cheeks were my mother's favorite summer meal and even though there was no chance that we might fry one up tonight, my grandfather loved me as much as any grandfather had ever loved his wild unreliable unpredictable grandchild.

The next time I saw those children, as we passed each other in the halls of the school designed to exalt them, we didn't speak.

There are moments that keep themselves in our memories: unexpected flashpoints of meaning we don't even recognize until the years, loves, worries have tempered the cloudy chatter of everyday concerns and have left only the brightest flashes: permanent, unchanging images that will most conspicuously blaze at that final, brilliant moment when our lives are said to pass before our dimming eyes.

Some speak of memories of fond, beloved days, of green lawns and blue skies, of smiling brides and laughing children, of the most tender instances of feeling loved, the most cherished moments of feeling protected, the most comforting interludes of feeling safe. Some speak of memories of daring times, of reaching for the rope of survival swinging above the abyss and catching it, gripping it, holding on for what became the rest of one's dear life. Others speak of moments that haunt and weep and cringe, that remind us always that we are and always will be victims of the ever-present past, that we are and always will be frightened of the dark, or of being alone, or, most frightening of all, of again being hunted by the unnamed blurred face that tracks us from dream to every dream and through each sweaty waking moment until we take our last never-ending breath.

The moments that have stayed with me comfort as well as haunt, and for the most part their meaning has escaped me. Asked to formulate a list of significant moments, moments that changed my life, I would hesitate to include that seemingly unremarkable afternoon when my grandfather approached me and those summer-day children on the Juneau docks. By then, I'd experienced times, images, moments, that had immediately and irrevocably clung to my thoughts, forcing my young mind to acknowledge even in its innocence that it had already begun to accumulate pictures of a confused, confusing life—not to make sense of them, not to sort, not to process, only to keep.

And what to make of the flash of an image of myself as a girl no more than four or five years old, resting on my haunches under the wooden table in the old kitchen, which in my memory is lit by one bare bulb, indicating winter; during summer's long days my grandmother let the electricity be turned off until the end of cannery season, when, rich again by our own standards, she could pay off the electric company and once again count the days until winter, when winter's long dark nights returned.

The end of summer, with its extra cash, was also the time to plan for celebrations. The old-style potlatches had been forbidden and replaced by legal congregations in churches along the shoreline and in bars along South Franklin Street. When the bars closed or got too rowdy for the bartender's taste, my grandmother, grandfather, and some of their friends would walk down Willoughby Avenue onto Village Street all the way to the edge of the village and come inside our old house, where sons and daughters would either be there waiting or they would not, where my uncles and aunts would either be home or would be gone, where I, only daughter of the oldest girl, I the youngest child, I the next generation, would be waiting there either hungry or not, but always curious, always watching, always ready to learn.

My memory contains the movement of a chair tossed across the floor, its velocity broken by another chair behind which I huddle and watch. No voices narrate my memory, no sounds complete the image. Only the thought of a young girl peeking out from under the wooden table, hiding herself for her own safety. Only a young girl learning how to act. Only a girl learning who to be.

A Raven woman places a borrowed Shungukeidí button blanket on my shoulders. As I walk down the aisle, I catch the eye of my proud son and his children. After alumni and politicians present speeches, I approach the podium. As I introduce myself in the Lingít language, someone in the audience calls a response. Whoever it is, I understand that he is proud: proud not of me, perhaps not even of my clan, the Kaagwaantaan. The power of these words of introduction has made a man proud of himself.

After the ceremony, I find the Raven woman and place money in her hand to restore balance between us.

Balance between opposite sides, Eagle and Raven, replicates the balance of life. Although capitalism and the church have changed old ceremonies and have left only form in many places where once there was substance, this essential balance continues to be realized in simple, private acts. After I retrieved my mother's ashes at the Fairbanks airport from a representative of what was then Alaska's only crematorium, who took the solemn occasion to remark that he had never before been called to deliver ashes to the bereaved at the airport, that he usually simply mailed them by the reliable postal service; after running my mother's ashes through some sort of scanner in those pre-9-11 days, the ashes showing as a heavy plastic bag of dense dark unidentifiable material that puzzled the clerk, to whom I had to say, Those are my mother's ashes; after I carried my mother's ashes on my lap back to Juneau; after I called everywhere for a bentwood box, preferably one carved by someone from the Raven side, in which to place my mother's ashes; after arranging an opportunity for those few people who remembered her from those long-lost village days to come see her smiling picture and the painted box in which her ashes now rested; after the few of us who were family walked to Evergreen Cemetery; after my mother's brother Eugene and my mother's grandchildren carrying in their arms her great-grandchildren, some of us with partners to support us in our grief, had assembled at the family plot, it fell to me to place her ashes in that bentwood box into the ground and cover my mother with the rich dirt in which her mother and her grandmother and two of her brothers rested and I could not.

A Raven held his bereaved opposites in his thoughts and offered comfort. As Eagles watched, a Raven covered their beloved sister, their cherished grandmother, my precious mother, with that rich dirt. A Raven heard my cry song, he opened the ground for her ashes, he carried my loved one to her grave. *Gunalchéesh.*

✦ ‖ ✦

More than mosses creep about on one patch of comforting earth. Voles scurry. Red squirrels scold. Deer mice listen.

Budworms are on the hunt. Sawflies wander, spiders spin. A snail keeps away from a hopping jay. So does his neighbor, the worm. They climb through sweet-scented stalks of violet and blushing petals of dogwood, dodging beetles and falling leaves. Mother-care plant gets ready to be made into fragrant tea.

Do you smell the fragrance of berry bushes in the spring, the fragrance of summer's wet soil, the fragrance of fall sockeye becoming older in the creek? Everything on our fragrant scrap of earth knows when the time is right to make its move. Everything counsels us to recognize when the time is ripe to move, and then to move.

Do everything in its order when all is ready. When all is ready, do not delay. When the time presents itself, move fast like the north wind in winter. When the natural order is clear, be impenetrable like the densest summer forest. When the time has come to make your move, be relentless like the river in the spring when the glacier is thawing and the snow is melting and the clouds are backed up against the rainshadow and pouring out their heavy water so they can lift themselves over the mountains in their own good time. Take each certain step in its proper order. Do not allow yourself to hesitate.

Take Raven. When it was time to be born, he was born. After he had listened, after he had studied his circumstances, when it was time for him to be born, Raven was born. He did not allow himself to hesitate. These are the steps that Raven took to achieve his goal.

More than leaves fall upon this softened scrap of earth. Some say that deaths come when leaves fall, but life falls onto the ground as well. All good things fall to the ground in their natural order. The drop of water from the leaf, the leaf itself, the limb, the branch, the tree. The comfortable cabin. The resolute woman, the mother, the child.

Can you taste the life that is hidden and buried and cries and covers and falls? Everything upon our scrap of earth is life itself. Everything teaches that we do our best when we are in agreement with our conditions.

Avail yourself of helpful circumstances. When circumstances have combined to offer you a position beyond defeat, occupy it decisively. After you are safe, find an even more advantageous place to improve your position. Victory is kind to the ones who seek their victory with careful calculations.

Take Raven. He pressed his grandfather for each box, for each box, for each box. When his position led him to each new plaything with which to improve his situation, he took advantage of his circumstance. With careful calculation, Raven obtained the final prize and gave us daylight. From that gift, the morning light now reveals a scrap of earth out of which come the taste of berries, the smell of cedar, the raven's cry. Into that scrap of earth one resolute woman will gladly return. *I gú.áax x'wán.* We take heart.

The mission of waging life calls for us to keep our weapons sharp. Although few now go into daily battle with swords drawn and bayonets set, we must all meet life as it unfolds before us, with our qualities sharpened or dull, our abilities at the ready or unprepared, our skills razor-like or blunted. No matter if we are not ready, no matter if we feel the need for another moment, another day, another long while for our planning. Life will come at us when the time for the event has arrived. Even though we can't unfailingly predict our next challenge, we can help to make ourselves as ready as possible by keeping our weapons sharp. All wise people, all who survive, all living things, are governed by this advice. Every good thing from which we learn does not fail to recommend this rule.

Take Raven. At that time when he needed to find entry but instead was confronted by an old man's invincible house, he didn't approach the unassailable structure with a dull adze and unsharpened knife. No. He sharpened his skills. He made the blade of his calculations as keen and as quick as the cutting edge of the deadliest dagger. Or perhaps—as, after all, he was Raven—the knife after which he modeled the sharpness of his cunning had been fashioned from jade. Or he may have arrived at the house come recently from a visit to the neighbors and cousins and in-laws, not far from the land over which he had recently flown, spitting water, and over which he would soon fly again, chasing stars, chasing the moon, chasing the sun, and perhaps he was carrying with him the vision of a blade of sharpest black slate. No matter. We may never truly know, until perhaps the knowledge is given to an artist, to a totem carver, to a weaver, to a dagger maker, to a painter, to a storyteller, and we read knowledge from that craftsperson's vision. In the meantime, we can only be certain that whatever the material from which Raven fashioned his strategy, he kept his cunning sharp and did not allow his weapons to become dull.

And we can take heart from his example. When his exploits had brought him as far as they could go, when his deceptions were finally in plain sight, when his shrewdness had been all but spent, nevertheless he was still quick to make his move. His weapons had remained sharp, his resourcefulness had not been dulled. With the sharp blade of his lively inclinations, he squeezed himself through the smokehole and emerged to give light to the world.

But starlight and moonlight and daylight are not the only gifts that Raven gave to the world, and gripping in his beak the summer-berry-red light of day was not the only time that, after calculated contractions, he had thrust himself through a smokehole and brought more life to the world. With cunning and trickery, he had once done the same with fresh water, had fooled another old man, had fully prepared for that old exaltation and shame, whereupon that old man had turned Raven's feathers from brilliant expectant white to breathtaking black. By the sharpness of his cunning, Raven escaped, and from his beak there drifted and streamed rivers and lakes and abundant waterfalls.

Raven teaches that we can be both devious and practical at the same time. His teachings are open lessons, for we suspect that the way to living an open life cannot be examined by a closed mind. Raven's teachings are open, so it is difficult for us to comment upon them aloud. They cannot easily be named.

⊹ ❘ ⊹

We huddled together on that gray April afternoon, generations of remnant Eagles and a Raven to hold us up and help us bury our loved one. Most of us at the gravesite had over and over endured the disorders visited upon us, and we had witnessed so many more. I handed the box that contained my mother's ashes to be consigned to the welcoming ground. I knew I would spend the rest of my life hoping to understand the choices she had made in this cultural war, a war that had befallen our family in her grandmother's generation and continued through my generation and beyond.

Intergenerational trauma does not produce dropout statistics and suicide rates. Intergenerational trauma produces heartbleed sweat tears bruises neglect hugs babykisses grief confusion raucous silence and love love love. It is the people who perpetuate the trauma—those who come to save, to study, to educate—who produce the failure-ridden statistics, the suicide rates, and the damning reports of all those good intentions gone wrong yet again, good intentions paving freshly landscaped, bulldozed roads to hell.

To my great-grandmother came the redeemers with this announcement: We bring to you the good news that everything you hold true, everything passed to you from generation to generation since Time Immemorial, all the philosophy and history and meaning of life that you and your ancestors have contemplated and considered and studied throughout your generations, all that you have believed, is untrue and indeed is full of something we call sin, sin that comes from a being we call Satan, the devil himself. All things that come from Satan, which is all the worldly pleasure that we call sin, offends someone we call God, and the Son of God, who was born without the earthly pleasure that is one of the many things that we call sin. All this and so many other sins, both known and yet unknown, which we will reveal to you as we go along, will send you headlong to a place that we call Hell, which is a place that the one that we call God has made especially for anyone who will not do as is commanded and as is translated by us in what we call the Word of God and is commanded by the manifest laws and rules of the people destined to come after us in the name of the Holy Father, who has told us that if you do not give up your beliefs and your savage ways of life—your land, your language, your art, and all your riches—you will without doubt be on your way to the place prepared for you by our loving God, that place we call Hell, where you will burn for all eternity, world without end. Amen.

The genius of colonialism is that it delivers immediate benefit to the people who designed the system as well as those who are privileged by its unbalance, and it ensures long-term dividends to their children and grandchildren— the sort of dividends that arrive unacknowledged and unchallenged, accompanied by the message that it was hard work that blessed these fortunates with their earned destinies—hard work and the undeniable condition of being extra special. No need to give any thought to the fact that a society constructed to send the message that one group is superior guarantees that other groups will receive the message that they are inferior. After all, if they can build a country on a foundation of genocide and slavery and call it the land of the free, they can certainly tell themselves they've worked for everything they have. As did their parents, they might say. As did their grandparents, they would certainly believe. And back and back and back through their own counted generations, all the way back to whoever it was that answered the siren's offer of rich land free to any white man not afraid of hard work. And any white woman willing to sit by his side, ready to teach her unwashed sisters how to be clean, ready to teach her downtrodden sisters how to mother their unfortunate children, ready to teach everyone who can be forced to listen why enjoying worldly pleasures is a sin, why all the ways that have been in place for generation upon generation must now be destroyed, and why a white man's education is the way to that good place.

Indian boarding schools in the United States were established with the purpose of converting, assimilating, and Americanizing Indigenous people. In Alaska, some of these schools served the purposes of public schooling and were run by the government, and some were run by religious organizations and housed children who had been removed from their homes. Some schools actively discouraged elements of Native culture such as language, art, and ceremonies, some actively enforced Christian practices, and few if any provided a curriculum that allowed a Native child to take pride in any aspect of being Native. These children attended these schools in the 1940s, 1950s, and 1960s, and were given the clear message that in order to be civilized they must forget their Native identity, convert to Christianity, and in most cases be vocationally educated in a service occupation. The children who attended these schools lost their Native language, lost their Native identity, and lost their Native history. It's no surprise that many of the students in those formative years came out of their educational experience with little or even no knowledge of their culture. It's no surprise that many of the students in those formative years came out of their educational experience with little or even no sense of self-worth. It's no surprise that many of those students came out of their educational experience with little or even no parenting skills. The surprise is that Native people are still here at all.

The traumatic effect of the national policies of Manifest Destiny, removal, assimilation, and conversion is undeniable. When a seemingly endless and overpowering force of people confronts a group of people already in place with the articulated purpose of destroying their culture, the inescapable result is cultural trauma. The only question might be how long the destruction will take.

For cultures that were in existence for thousands and tens of thousands of years, it's reasonable to expect that when they are dealt a killing blow—a killing blow delivered over a span of fifty to sixty years—the death, even a speedy one, will take three or four generations. When seen in that light, we can recognize that the symptoms we bemoan—incarceration, suicide, alcoholism, high-school dropout, college dropout, smoking, early pregnancy, depression, tuberculosis, poverty, removal of children, abuse, domestic violence, termination of parental rights, fetal alcohol syndrome—are symptoms of cultural trauma. We are witnessing what was intended to be the death throes of a culture. And as we do when we attend any death, we must do so with the constant knowledge that in spite of the agony, in spite of the great sorrow, in spite of the stink, we are witnessing something sacred.

It's helpful to examine the direct effects of trauma: confusion, memory loss, anger, guilt, fear, anxiety, withdrawal, disruptions in worldview. It's even more instructive to look at the secondary and associated effects of trauma: depression, isolation, despair. Hopelessness, loss of faith, self-destructiveness. Aggression toward others, lack of coping skills. Job problems, education problems, marital problems. Shame, self-blame, lack of trust. Detachment, disconnection, hostility, avoidance. Lack of interest. Identity issues. Low self-esteem. Feelings of worthlessness. Poor health. Alcohol and other dependency issues, together with all the problems that come with these behaviors.

The intended death throes of a culture.

It's useful to wonder what we would do if five years from now the American culture was suddenly subdued by another culture that believed theirs was the superior way of living, their god was the one true god, their language the only worthwhile speech, their history the only history that mattered. It's a helpful exercise to ask ourselves what would happen if this young American society suddenly was rocked by cultural trauma. It's almost unthinkable, but suspending our disbelief for a moment to consider what would happen to our grandchildren's children if in the span of the next fifty or sixty years a killing blow was delivered to the way of life we now know is an edifying challenge.

We would no longer be allowed to speak English. In schools, offices, stores—everywhere—all communication would be conducted in some new language we didn't understand.

Our laws would be swept away. No more regulations, acts of Congress, municipal codes, laws as we know them. Everything would be done according to some new legal system that we didn't understand and that was created and enforced in someone else's favor.

Our religions would be abolished. Bible studies and Communion and concepts like Manifest Destiny would be seen as prehistoric and evil. There would be no more "In God we trust" on our money. In fact, there would be no more money. The new currency would be in the hands of others. Our wealth—our bank accounts, our property, our belongings—would suddenly be of no value to us, and most of our remaining fortunes would be taken from us.

Our standards of beauty would be ridiculed. Our art would be trivialized. All of our place names would be changed. Our own names would be changed. We would be forced to celebrate peculiar holidays that glorify acts committed against us. Our children would be taken from us and sent far away, where they would be forced to forget English, forced to dress in someone else's fashions, and forced to learn trades that prepared them for servitude. Taken from our influence, they would be given unpronounceable new names in a foreign language, they would not learn the history of their country, they would not know who they were related to, and they would receive the strong message that whatever they did, they would never be as good as those who were members of the dominant culture. Taken from us at early ages, they would not learn how to parent. Their children would receive the same negative cultural messages. Before long, no one would be learning English as a first language. Before long, our legal and educational and spiritual and social systems and beliefs would disappear. Before long, only a few old ones would remember how it used to be.

In time—just a few years beyond that—a resurgence of interest in traditional American culture would occur. After all the land had been taken and all the art destroyed and all the worldviews that it took 250 years for this country to develop had been finally done away with, it would become fashionable for people to confess they were part American. The few people remaining who spoke English as a first language would be studied. The old photographs that had been hidden away would be brought out for interpretation. Most of the cultural artifacts, including most of those photos, would already be in museums, where they would be visited by curious tourists trying to remain open-minded about such quaint ways of life. Christian artifacts would be considered beautiful but primitive. People belonging to the then-dominant culture would become recognized authorities on the American. Some scholars and would-be authorities would even claim an American identity. Those who were truly part American would possess the least authority in all things, including all things American. Those who were truly part American would be incarcerated, would drop out of school, would lose their children to new laws, would abuse themselves with whatever addictive drugs were then available, would suffer poverty, depression, anger, shame, suicide, domestic violence, and all the other inevitable effects of cultural trauma. There would be no lack of reports and meetings and task forces studying the problems of their failed assimilation. Once in a while a part American whose grandmother spoke English but whose mother did not, who had managed to obtain a colonizer's education later in life, who worried over her children and grandchildren but didn't know what to do besides go on, would manage against all odds to capture a position at a colonial institution and at the end of her life would wonder if she had done any good, or if there was even any good that could have been done.

I trace my family's trauma at least to my great-grandmother Anna Willard, whose most significant trauma, as for so many in those days of the first colonial onslaught, was the loss of an Indigenous belief system in her conversion to Christianity. My understanding is that too many of that generation and the next fell victim to the first wave of what was to be the never-ending assault, the push to subdue, to convert, to oppress, to educate, to condemn. The first killing weapon was always the Good News.

⊩ ‖ ⊩

Raven found a grandfather in that old house at the top of the Nass River, a grandfather to love him as a grandparent loves a grandchild. In his love, that grandfather stands in for all grandparents, and he stands in for more than that one thing. That grandfather stands in for everything we might want to learn about what might happen to us when we enter that ancient world. But there is also a grandmother who can help us know what to expect, a grandmother who can teach us what we might be forced to learn, a grandmother who can tell us about things that might happen after we find ourselves in a new world. Just like Raven's grandfather, this grandmother's understanding has been tested many times. And this grandmother's heart has been broken more than once.

To succeed in the white man's world, that grandmother might have at last persuaded herself that she would take up the white man's tools. She might already have spent fifty years in unproductive rebellion, eschewing such artificial measures as financial security, home ownership, career. She would turn away from spending whole afternoons on barefoot walks in dewed clover, from whiling away the morning sitting on a comfortable boulder alongside a chatty creek, from ciphering the rubbed-out letters on a fallen gravestone. She would turn away from ringing the bell at a favorite downtown bar, from sidewise glances at likely and unlikely men, from laughing with homeless friends at tourists who have lost their way and are now asking how best to find the nearest jewelry store, the closest T-shirt place, the cheapest gift shop that features grotesquely painted sharp-toothed blasphemies that tourists don't care were produced by foreign machines dialed to carve out five-inch monstrosities that are then labeled totems and shipped off to Alaska. This was, after all, the trip of their lifetimes, the grandmother could have assured herself, and the Native artifacts that tourists paid to see were displayed in museums and underneath glass counters, not sitting on the dock passing lukewarm beer in bottles hidden by brown paper sacks and telling each other stories of their real lives, stories not meant for anyone but themselves and those others who had also lived through those years. That grandmother must have turned away from all these unsuccessful pleasures and pastimes, and she must have determined to get herself to the white man's college for a chance at success in the white man's world.

It could have been a grandmother's second year in college when out the front window of her decades-old but proudly purchased mobile home, there on the graveled driveway might have stood an Eagle grandchild with his mother.

Having perhaps only seen that grandchild at irregular holidays, happenstance birthdays, and chance bump-ins at any local store or on the city bus, that grandmother must have been curious at the recent goings-on. She had probably not known they were homeless. She had most likely not known they'd been couch-surfing in the houses of friends and what seemed an infinite number of cousins, until they'd worn out their welcome in every place and walked over to her front yard. At any rate, just as that old man welcomed his unplanned Raven grandson, that grandmother must have settled her own Eagle grandchild in one of the bedrooms, his mother in the other, and arranged herself a sleeping place on the living room couch. She must have delighted once again in her grandchild's thoughtful tenderness, his toddling desire to please. She must have pretended to chase him down the narrow hall, catching him and spinning his dreams and her hopes into the thin, hungry air.

In that home's attached, dirt-floor garage, that grand-mother had stored a wealth of treasures, including jars of bent and rusted nails, piles of worn-out doormats and odd-shaped carpet remnants, broken chairs, three-legged tables, boxes of paper memories—love letters, grocery lists, warped photos—and a transparent two-person tent that had never been used for camping, which she set up in the side yard only for the grandchild's solemn pleasure.

His smile delighted her. He was, after all, her first and only grandchild, the one who had appeared like a pine needle floating in a cup, unbidden but not unloved. He had been born, she had counted his toes and listened to his parents' promises, they had shared a few family holidays, and then he had drifted away on predictable tides. When young parents drift apart, the child is pulled along. The grandmother had lived through enough abandonment, had done her share of abandoning, and she knew that, like the tide, she had good reason to hope that she might see her grandchild again.

Like the tide, she knew he might come and go, and so he did.

Later that day that grandmother found two cans of whipped cream hidden under a thin blanket on the tent floor, splotches drying on the blue tarp, along with a few broken crackers and puddles of spilled juice. She remembered her cousin Esther, who also used to hide food, in Esther's case, carrots and radishes from the garden and cold fried hens that had met their fate when they stopped laying daily eggs. That grandmother remembered her own bouts with the food that her own mother had packed into her grade-school lunch boxes, the lovingly prepared food that she would only just nibble on then give to her only friend, the one other girl in the classroom who also lived in the downtown Indian Village. Or she would take the barely bitten crusts and uneaten apple slices home in the pail to hide from her mother. Until one day her mother met her unexpectedly as she barreled out of school. Walking down the stairs that led to their part of town, she had crafted an elaborately unbelievable lie about how her only friend had snuck into the coat closet with an exactly similar lunch and come back out with an empty pail and no one knew or could even guess where Lorraine's food had gone. It was truly a mystery, she assured her mother. It was truly a marvel.

Her mother punished her somehow—she now imagines it was by condemning her to her narrow room off the kitchen, where she could hear her mother explaining to her favorite uncle why he wasn't to joke and play and visit her that day. Her mother could only have been confused and hurt. Her mother knew how hard it was to work long enough to afford the sandwich makings, a banana, a cookie, a carton of milk, and to put them in a colorful lunch pail so a little girl from the village, that little girl who would one day be a grand-mother, could be just as good as any of the other little girls. What that mother didn't want to know was that it would take more than store-bought white bread and peanut butter to make that little girl feel as though she was just as good as all the other girls in her grade. What that little girl didn't yet know was that being hurt was her mother's only defense and it was her mother's strongest weapon.

That little girl, now a grandmother, must have thought about these things when she found the whipped cream in the tent, but her main impression must have been irritation at having to clean up the melting mess in the humid tent in the afternoon of a rare sunny day. She must have marched her grandson into the kitchen and told that charming child once again that he could have anything that was in the refrigerator or in the cupboard, that they would go to the store the next day for more of his favorite things, and that she just needed to know what he took so she could keep track of what to buy for him. "Yes, Grandma," he must surely have promised, the first of many promises he was without doubt destined to break.

✦ ‖ ✦

When I worked as a summer naturalist on the Alaska State ferries, I would occasionally tell the story about Raven and the Box of Daylight. "I never really understood this story," I would confess to the passengers, "until I became a grand-mother myself. Then I understood why Raven's grandfather gave him the Box of Daylight when he fussed for it." The pas-sengers would chuckle and nod their acknowledgment of our shared indulgent grandparents' love. "I tell my grandchildren I'll give them anything they ask me for, anything they want," I would go on. "I tell my grandchildren that if I could, I would even give them the Box of Daylight."

I would give my grandchildren a Box of Daylight. I would give them a Box of Moonlight. To my grandchildren, I would give the stars.

⊹ ‖ ⊹

Inside that old man's darkened house inside that darkened world, boxes of light are not the only wealth. Although the value of each carved box, of each protective crest, of each set of many eyes and teeth guarding the light can never be counted, nevertheless the boxes number themselves among the cabin's other riches.

That old man's house rests upon welcoming earth worn smooth by the passage of so many steps over so many generations they cannot be counted. Polished platforms repeat the shape of the house and surround a center fire. Along the walls, woven curtains enclose sleeping places for relatives and friends should they ever find a way to enter. Should they ever find the way to enter. When they finally are ready to come inside.

At the back of the house, a tall screen looms. The figures on the screen change shape with each glimpse, with each gaze, with each vision. Who is to say what crest adorns the screen that Raven saw? What person can say what form embellishes the screen that they themselves will see? Who can describe the shape of the screen that anyone will see? We can only say that there, at the back of the seemingly impenetrable house that Raven managed to pierce, a tall screen looms.

Behind the screen, Raven's grandfather has always kept the most valuable of his riches, including those priceless boxes of light. Furs from people who were not yet animals, who were still animals, who would soon be our animal relatives. Shells given to that old man by a man even older than himself, a man at ease on the water, an old man unafraid to paddle so far beyond the shore that only fog can be seen. Fog and occasional wanderers who have drifted too far from the coast. In other precious boxes behind that precious screen, blankets woven in the most intricate style, blankets that dance, blankets that tell stories. Blankets that embody relation to the land. Relation to the water. Relation to one another. Beads that have traveled from places farther than even Raven can fly in one long day. Songs from the people who live in those far places. Carved boxes that contain things too splendid for our mind's eye. Carved boxes that enclose incredible things, too improbable for us to believe. Carved boxes that contain treasures that will astonish us far more than ordinary things like brilliant daylight, utter moonlight, light from the grandest stars.

On the face of the screen, a spider waits.

TWO

Wolves Sing like Old Women
Keeping Ancient Songs

O NE OF THE DREAMS that eventually, inevitably, pulled me back to Alaska was the romantic no-tion—one still shared by so many in this country— of building my own place to live at the edge of the forest, on Indian land. The congressional act that freed the North Slope from its land freeze and opened it for oil exploration had been passed in 1971 when I was living in California, trapped in a double-wide trailer anchored to parched ground behind double-locked gates, surrounded by obstinate cattle, jack-in-the-box grasshoppers, and sunbathing rattlesnakes, the dust-filled dry road that connected the cattle-gate to our front door holding no promise of any way out.

Upon that act of Congress that seemed at the time to guarantee Alaska Native people ownership of land, I built my dream. The fact that its inflated promises turned out to be the equivalent of twenty-four dollars' worth of beads and trinkets, while the newly formed Native corporation sent ir-regular notices of its new-fashioned building, extolling its grand furnishing and carpets, the dozens of directors and at-torneys and consultants it had engaged to uphold my rights not as an individual nor as a member of a clan, but as part of the counted conglomerate—dissuaded me only during those infrequent rational moments when I blinked, recognized my misery, and once more looked away to dream of freedom from the daily tantrums and disapproval thrust into my life by the ill-tempered man toward whom some years before I'd so predictably drifted. I imagined myself without him, living in the damp forest where cockroaches and grasshoppers and oak worms and rattlesnakes were not to be found, where rain and wind washed and nurtured salmon and blueberries, where the worst outburst a woman could fear was from a bad-tempered brown bear, the cousin with whom I could sometimes reason and from whom I could always hide.

I would choose a patch of land not far from a traveled road yet close to a stream, close to the beach, securely snuggled at the edge of the sheltering woods. For maximum daylight and to ensure I would not have to cut down too many trees, my homesite would be situated on the edge of a sunny clearing. That choice would probably also ensure the presence of berries. But the presence of berries would also guarantee the presence of bears. Even when building a life in my imagination, it turned out, I couldn't avoid problems. But a daydream solution was always at hand, and for the bears I relied on the lessons my grandmother had taught me long ago. I would talk to the bear, I would let him know that we were relatives, I would ask him to feel sorry for me and to let me share these ripened berries, of which I wanted only a few and no more than my share, and he would be certain not to harm me. Instead, he would turn away, curious, perhaps bad-tempered, but deterred by the confession of our kinship, and I would finish picking a serving-size basket of summer berries to provide me energy enough to continue building my little home on this one small scrap of earth.

Clearing a patch of land is no easy thing. When I was a girl, I would often hike over the bridge to the Douglas side to visit Aunt Erm and her husband, Uncle George, who, to my movie-struck eyes, looked just like the hero of the day, the man whom all moviegoers were trained to admire, John Wayne, the great Indian-fighter who stood for all things American and all things good. Uncle George, himself a white man, was never visibly flattered by my comparisons. Over the years, I learned, he'd claimed land along the Juneau side of Douglas Island, had built houses, carved out gardens, and for some reason unexplained to me had packed up and moved ever northward along the shore, ever closer to the Juneau-Douglas bridge, which local memory testified had been built some ten years before I was born. In only a few years, I was old enough to walk from the Juneau village across the windy bridge and then another half-mile southward along the narrow two-lane road, down the hairpin-tiered, dirt-covered, wooden stairway that opened to the sight of the barely plumbed house at the edge of the beach below. The already green front garden leafed in rows of turnips, beets, potatoes, allowing just a glimpse of the back garden and its promise of almost-ripe peas and peppery sweet nasturtiums. Across the channel, Juneau rested along the base of the fresh clean face of Mt. Roberts, which with Mt. Juneau eclipsed every church, every school, every store, every street, every alley built along that narrow coastal strip across the channel.

To me, the bridge between Juneau and the road to Aunt Erm's house was only an often chilly, often lonely place where

I could stand at the highest curve and measure the steps between me and the promise of Aunt Erm's fried chicken and gravy, and wonder if Esther, George's daughter, would be home or if she would once again have run away. Perhaps she was hiding now under the wood risers or holed up in the abandoned house two properties south, sneaking carrots from the garden and water from the well, cold but happy to be out of the house, calling to me as I explored rocks along the beach, luring me into the dank, empty house to reenact with me what must have driven her from the house, not unlike Dolly, my grandmother's youngest child, when she was forced to drag me along on her own promiscuous adventures.

I was never witness to Uncle George clearing the land or planting the houses' foundations. By the time I arrived, he'd built his last homesteaded house, its first floor a bit higher than the ground, up a couple of stairs to the front washroom entry, where eggs and the paraphernalia for their care were piled around the only place where water was piped into the house, a sink at which we washed the bits of yellowed straw and dried chickenshit off the morning's eggs, weighed them, separated them into cartons, and stacked them to be delivered for sale as Heinkel's Cackleberries. We set aside the eggs with broken shells, oversized jumbos, and tiny-baby peewees to be stirred into Aunt Erm's exotic layered and frosted cakes, whipped into her fluffy dinner omelets, and hard-boiled for her fresh-from-the-garden green salads.

I was always afraid of the chickens when it was my turn to collect the eggs. I was always afraid of Esther. I was always afraid of Dolly. I was afraid of children on the playground and wary of children on the street, afraid of teachers who were so foreign to my experience, apprehensive of doctors and dentists and uniformed men. I was afraid of everything I suspected to be part of the truth of my existence. With most of these dangers, I knew I could never reason, but from them all I knew I could somehow always hide.

Clearing the land might be a difficult thing to do and I undoubtedly inexperienced, but in my imagination there were no boulders to move, no tree stumps to pull, very little that needed to be flattened and nothing that needed to be killed. Smoothing the site would be like sweeping my arm across a ruffled bolt of silk, a tent nearby, under a tall spruce, sheltering me from rain and cold reality. The land to clear would be nothing like the land in California where I had been trapped for too many years. No barbwire blackberry bushes covering the ground in every direction, no slow-witted cows dropping pie-bombs underfoot, no dust-storm sun baking and sweating and sucking away all life, all energy, all hope. Only a few salmonberry bushes, only an ice-cold stream. Only the dream of a safe tomorrow. Only the promise of rain.

✦ ‖ ✦

After the missionaries, armed with their promises of heaven and their threats of eternal hell, came soldiers armed with guns and killing machines. The plain recognition of life everywhere was traded for the dream of life everlasting. The United States was nearing the end of what they liked to call the Indian Wars, and bombing a handful of villages along with threatening to bomb a few others proved to be at least as effective as any army of missionaries. After those onslaughts, designed to terrify and subdue, the next assault was conducted by enlisted white women, carrying with them the civilized printed word they labeled education, along with an unquestioned presumption of civilized housekeeping, illustrated by sketches of yellow-haired women dressed in white frilled aprons holding platters of white bread and processed sugar. Armed with false claims of cleanliness produced by washed floors and unwashed hands, they admitted beauty only in their own reflections. They meant well. After all, none could deny that in the old as well as the newly Christian worlds, nothing is quite so tempting, so irresistible, as the forbidden sins that now must be wiped as clean as the tiles upon which we walk and upon which no reasonable man or woman would care to serve or eat a dinner.

The Bureau of Indian Affairs didn't get serious about sending Juneau children to boarding schools until several years after people moved to the Indian Village part of town. At first, Native children were compelled to attend the Indian school in Juneau, and then as the town grew, one school accommodated all the town's children who didn't attend the Catholic school. Native children in every family must have come home with stories they'd heard from their teachers, stories of Christmas and Easter and roast turkeys and apple pies, reinforced by churchly mandates of solemn celebration. Always happy for a chance to throw a feast, for almost two generations my grandmother did her best to make a turkey on the day Native people were told to call Thanksgiving, and she even listened with care to stories of how the white man's god had brought white people to this new land that the white man's god had told them they were meant to subdue. According to the preachers and the schools, everyone was supposed to give thanks for that heavenly deed, even the people whose land it had been before the white man's god stepped in and decided to help the white children he so loved take all the land from the Indian children he so loved. Nevertheless, a winter feast was a winter feast, and after it became against the church's teachings and against accepted practices to hold the winter ceremonies that white men called potlatches, the new holidays were about the only hope for a winter celebration, so everyone had to make do with decorating a withering tree with paper snowflake doilies.

The new laws also made it almost impossible for people who lived in the Juneau Indian Village to catch and dry fish or to shoot deer, so most families kept a pretty slim cupboard. Some families had no young men in the outlying villages from whom they could expect sheets of half-dried salmon or fresh halibut steaks or a shoulder of smoked deer meat or servings of black seaweed and herring eggs. The food that relatives brought along when they came to town to visit usually was enough to cover what they ate while they were in town. My grandfather fished on a commercial boat, so he didn't bring much home. And a lot of the money he did bring home from fishing, and the money my grandmother brought home from cannery work, went to the South Franklin Street bars and to the City Café when they felt rich. When they were lucky, they got a free Thanksgiving turkey courtesy of the church's spirit of charity, and sometimes another turkey from the church a white man's month later to celebrate the holy wonder of virgin birth.

Let us imagine the bounty: nothing so grand as an ear of corn that can't be grown in the temperate rain forest. Nothing so tasty as pink, canned beef-like substance, nothing so fresh as wilted civilized lettuce taking its god-given rightful place on the breakable bone china instead of the savage wild greens grown sweet and tangy in the spring meadow and throughout the summer's forested, shadowed edge. After the missionaries who sent our souls to their own heaven as well as to god's own hell came soldiers who sent our fathers to war and our sons to prison. After them came the white women, who sent our children to boarding schools and summer camps where they heard our own old stories told by someone visiting from somewhere three thousand miles away, encouraging a schoolboy to play a violin, revealing her conviction that chamber music was the way to soothe the one she thought was a savage beast but whom we knew was our cousin. And after all that came the lawyers to sell our land and everything on it, to make our land no more than figures on corporate balance sheets, to measure out our birthright in dollar-sign dividends, now that we have become the shareholders they have taught us to be, now that we are consumer-shareholders in service of their manifest colonial destiny. Now that the corporate income statement only adds to our many, many losses.

How best to plead for who we might have been had it not been for colonial invasion, how best to condemn the all-form no-substance shell made in their own god's own image? Serve to us a dish of self-righteous greed, sprinkle it with Indian policy, garnish it with early-bird trinkets smothered with multimillion losses, offer it with platitudes and a generous side of sanctimonious you-people. Scrape what's left off the corporate patent leather shoe. The corporation owns our land. The corporation charges us an entrance fee to admire their display of our culture's treasures. The corporation requires us to pay to dance in their Celebration. The corporation brings non-Native scholars from other places to lecture us about why our relatives' ceremonies were once against the law. Chiefs sold their daughters into prostitution, a lettered woman explains to an audience come here to listen to a European scholar in Alaska for a few weeks to research Tlingit art and history. She suggests that the meaning of an object is measured by the way its collectors perceive it.

She is wrong. Everything has spirit. Inherent meaning enlivens all things, whether or not cultural thieves can understand. I turn away, but not before she perceives my pointless disdain, not before she disapproves of my desperate, impotent anger.

⊹ ‖ ⊹

We all know that Raven plotted the theft of his grandfather's wealth. That grandmother, the one who knows us and knows our world, could not have thought she would be able to escape what that grandfather had not been able to avoid.

Perhaps it was late in the summer, perhaps it was the beginning of fall, when on a weekend afternoon of another rare day of pleasant breezes and bright warm sun, someone crept into that old grandmother's kitchen with the slightest of quiet sounds. Since her grandson had just left with his visiting mother to walk to a shallow pond in the nearest expanse of forest, that grandmother must have told herself that one of them had come back for a forgotten snack to take along. When that grandmother wandered toward the front of the house, no one was there.

All the lamps and ceiling lights were turned off during bright summer days; the sunlight beating down on the dirt driveway must have warned her of the heat she had never loved. Rather, she loved the cool shaded cloudy promise of rain. Rather, she loved the sound of distant voices reminding her that she could be alone in her own house while not alone in this life. Rather, she loved to know about children's plans to run, to walk, to wander, and herself to find a reason to stay home.

In a bid for better education and a stronger chance for habit and discipline, that grandson, for the few years he had lived with his grandmother, had attended daily home-school tutoring sessions and weekly karate classes. For those costly activities, that grandmother put all her coins and single dollars into a jar on the shelf and made up the difference every week. She supported herself and her grandchild on a limited income, student loans, and summer work, and together with irregular grants and minor dividends from local tribal organizations, that grandmother made do. Counting money and sending checks were rituals she followed each week, making sure the grandson watched and counted and helped. It reminded her of those old stories of Tlingit men and women when the twentieth century was in its infancy, those Tlingit grandmothers and grandfathers who were said to have saved every penny so they could donate to the Alaska Native Brotherhood and Alaska Native Sisterhood in their pursuit of compensation from the American government for their stolen land. Just as they had saved every penny, so did that grandmother save her pennies. They had saved every dollar and so did she. She reminded herself that it was all an investment in a hoped-for future, one that all those other grandparents knew they might never see.

By the time the United States reached Alaska, there was no more need for treaties, reservations, agreements, recognition, or negotiation. What the new people wanted they simply took, what they didn't want they destroyed. In response, the Alaska Native Brotherhood was established in 1912, to address the uncompensated loss of traditional lands and to pursue land claims for the illegal taking of most of Lingit Aani, eighteen million acres most people now call the Tongass National Forest. Among its express goals was assimilation, thought at the time to be the most likely road to justice. As part of that strategy, English was adopted as the Alaska Native Brotherhood's official language. Although their insistence of English, Christianity, and parliamentary procedure now seems questionable, no doubt their decisions were made after lengthy and vigorous debate. It cannot be denied that they were resisting as best they could. The ANB, with the powerful support of the Alaska Native Sisterhood, petitioned the Indian Claims Commission. Following a human pattern, every grandmother and grandfather placed pennies and dollars aside to buy their grandchildren's better future. Grandparents around the world follow that pattern and have always done so, whether by constructing an elaborate social order that empowers only their own generations, or by putting every sparc coin and every single dollar in a jar on a shelf in an unattended kitchen.

As soon as that grandmother walked into the kitchen she must have seen that the money jar had been emptied. It sat naked on the shelf, the picture of a future so often predictable, a future that was no more than a repetition of the recent past. Although far too common, it was a future that she must have hoped might somehow be avoided, its inevitability somehow shortened, its certainty somehow denied.

※ ‖ ※

With the promise of a better future bound up in a mandatory Western-style education, Indigenous people in the early twentieth century appeared to have no choice. Lose children all at once to boarding schools, or lose them little by little to daily assaults by textbooks and teachers. In both cases, it seemed that the path to white-defined success was to surrender most of the identity that hadn't yet been seized or destroyed, and to allow what remained to be distorted. After all, Indian education isn't designed to teach Native children to be white. Indian education is designed to teach Native children to want to be white. Indian education is built on the purported goal of assimilation, which turns out, like all of the actors on the colonial stage, to be no more than another abscess-ridden moneychanger trying on a pretty dress. Indigenous children drop out of Western-model schools at rates higher than all other groups, and for uncountable, unutterable reasons, many do not succeed according to the white man's terms. This doesn't mean that Indian education is failing. On the contrary, Indian education is succeeding at what it was designed to do: produce Native failure.

Speaking out, speaking up, resisting, protesting—these acts show the tenacity of a culture that has had its philosophic center all but destroyed, its ways of education all but obliterated, its language threatened, its sovereignty denied, its laws disregarded, its authority displaced, and its lands and stories appropriated. But the gates of colonialism have not prevailed against it. For a few generations, Alaska Native people stood at a precipitous brink, at the end of a path constructed out of someone else's history.

And now an Indigenous path will be carved.

✢ ❘ ✢

In the afternoon of a dark day we sat on folding chairs in the grade school auditorium and listened to orchestra music piped in on a loudspeaker. To prepare us for this special treat, the teacher had explained to us the various instruments employed to make the sounds of the woodwind chorus, the percussion rhythm, the string section, the brass and keyboard notes. She had shown to us the undeciphered lines and dots on sheets that she instructed us would guide the determined musical scholar to a favorite song. She'd tacked to the bulletin board faded pictures of tubas and violins and flutes. She'd played a song on the piano, picking out the tune to "America the Beautiful," a song we'd been taught the year before, a song the words to which I wanted to believe. "Land where our fathers died," I sang, trying to imagine a shadowed manly figure made significant and powerful by his untouchable absence and his pilgrim's death. No matter how hard I pushed, I never quite squeezed out the tears.

Down the line of folding chairs our teacher stepped, bending to whisper in the pink ears of each button-shirted boy and blush-kneed girl. I dared to imagine she would whisper in mine. When I tipped my chair, it threatened to fold. I gripped the unpadded seat with unmanicured hands and tried to keep still as she bent, whispered, straightened, stepped, bent, whispered, straightened, stepped. Taller than

Uncle Skip, thinner than Aunt Ida, patting her pincurled hair and hardly moving her carefully reddened lips, she personified a control as absent and baffling as my unknowable father. Little heels on her gleaming brown shoes. Scalloped collar on her starched and laundered blouse. Kick pleats on her shiny unwrinkled skirt. Everything that I was told in books, in movies, in magazines, that I should want to be. Everything I was told in all those places and in school, in church, in stores, that I would never be.

During our weekly class sessions, she told stories and played music associated with names like Beethoven, Brahms, Mozart. She sat at a piano and followed the unfolded sheets of staff and clef and bars, giving us to know that, as with all things superior, this art, as all true art, originated in Europe and had been transmitted to this land only by way of those whose ancestors had also originated there. Originating in Europe, they were pilgrims to America, and they were the fathers who had died in this land. The words to the song, we all understood, were "Land where *their* fathers died." "Land of *their* pilgrims' pride." As she stepped down the line, bending her ear to hear each child's whispered answer, I contained my eager response, my choice, the selection that would earn from her a smile, approval, acceptance.

I listened to the exchange when she asked the girl sitting on the chair next to me "What instrument do you want to play when you grow up?" and rehearsed my choice in my imagination. She straightened, stepped, bent. "What instrument do you want to play when you grow up?" she whispered, and, almost tongue-tied, I named the instrument I was certain would transform me into the girl I knew I needed to be, the girl who would grow into the woman upon whom a happy, acceptable life depended, and whispered into her perfumed ear, "The harp." She stood, and raising her penciled eyebrows with amusement, advised me instead to choose the piano. Harps were the instrument of angels, and angels wore clean white clothes.

I supposed I'd been a fool to think I could play such a heavenly contraption. My family never even went to church, except on Salvation Army Christmas afternoons when presents were distributed to needy children, and on Easter mornings when the expectation was for boiled eggs. No harps adorned either place, but the pictures of White Jesus and White Angels and a blue-eyed mother named White Mary made it clear that they too came from Europe, like everyone else except me and my family and all the Tlingit people in our village and in the town.

I filed away the teacher's advice in the catchall category of the unreadable mysteries by which teachers and judges and doctors possessed the enviable power to always, so accurately, point out my shortcomings.

My mother and I traveled to California by plane and Greyhound bus two months before my sixteenth birthday. We stopped in Seattle for a night, staying at a downtown hotel not far from the bus station, timidly taking advantage of room service, ordering two hamburgers and marveling at the price for something not nearly as good as the plate-size ground steak on toasted man-size buns that were a favorite back home, at the café called Laura Lee's, just around the corner from the tiny place in Ashenbrenners Cabins we shared with Aunt Pauline. After we ate our hotel-delivered meal, we turned on the room's black-and-white TV and watched the *Ed Sullivan Show*, just as we did back home on Sunday nights. We felt the distance. For my mother, it must have been welcome, anonymous relief. For me, everything was filled with the noise and dust and exciting dry dirt of the new here and now, and it was also filled with the wet clean memory of the place I'd always called home. It would be that way for me for twenty-five years.

After a cramped day and night on a noisy Greyhound bus, we arrived in California and signed up for a room in another downtown hotel, this one cheaper and with no room service, while my mother called around for apartments and schools and checked in with her job at the Bureau of Indian Affairs, where she was scheduled to begin work as a Clerk Class II in just over a week and a half. My mother wasn't sorry to leave Juneau. She had sworn she'd never go back. She was probably only a little resentful that the reason we had to leave was my obstinate delinquency. The local authorities had threatened to send me away again; I'd begun again to drink and smoke and run around and was now a ward of the state.

My mother had been glad to have a reason to say goodbye to Juneau. She never forgot the stinging disapproval she had endured when her pregnancy became obvious to clucking neighbors and gossip-mongering relatives, and she was still talking about it thirty years later when we finally moved back home. She never forgot the strength of will it took to hold her head high when people she thought were her friends crossed the street when they saw her wheeling a baby carriage their way. She called them out by name years later when they tried to say Hello, how've you been. Only one or two had remained true friends. Only her family had stood by her and loved the new baby no matter what. By the time we left for California, most of that family had died or disappeared, and her one or two friendships had been strained to the limit by their well-meaning advice. She put in for a transfer to California, and two plane tickets and a long bus ride later there we were. My mother only wished she could travel somewhere on her own, maybe to Montana or Missouri or Washington, DC. She'd always wanted to travel, and it was clear that she was tired to death of me and all my unwelcome antics.

⊹ ∥ ⊹

On a day before Mabel inserted herself into Patricia's life, Patricia's dad bundled their dirty sheets to the laundromat up the street and came back from the boat with a handful of candy and a bag of sugar. "Where's your mom?" he asked. Neither of them knew.

Patricia finally got over being sick, nibbled on balls of store-bought white bread rolled in sprinkled sugar, dressed herself in wrinkled clothes fresh from her daddy's errand, and walked herself to school. She couldn't give her dad a good answer. She didn't know where her mom was. She never knew where her mom was unless her mom was right there in the house and Patricia could see her. Sometimes Lucille was gone for days. When she came back, she'd let Patricia kiss her dry cheek and wipe her sweaty forehead and fetch her some cold beer and a few aspirin. Whenever Lucille was gone somewhere, Patricia never had an answer when her dad said where's your mom.

When Patricia got home from school one day, she found a note on the table. Looking for your Mom, it said. Fix your own food, it said. Lock the door. Don't know when I'll be back.

Mabel knocked on the door a few days later. "Who is it?" Patricia called. She didn't recognize the knock.

"It's Mabel, honey," came an unfamiliar voice.

It sounded like a white lady's voice. Patricia said nothing.

"Remember me? From church?"

Lucille made a habit of taking Patricia to church service around Easter morning and sometimes in the days and even in the nighttimes around Christmas. It wasn't the same Christmas as everybody else, but the moaning and incense and men dressed in skirts couldn't take away from the joy Patricia felt when Lucille held her hand through the whole long-winded service. Twice a year she went to another kind of church with her dad and her grandfather Old Tom. The people there were dressed in army clothes, right down to the policeman's hat and shiny buttons. They gave presents to all the children who were there and led them all down the stairs to the basement, where plates of frosted cookies and bowls of eggy potato salad and jars of smoky fish and pitchers of sweet yellow lemonade covered every table and with deep-colored red and green napkins invited everyone in the church to eat as much as they could possibly want. Patricia wanted to hold her daddy's hand, but she lost him in the crowd. She made herself sick with hardboiled mustard eggs and sweetened punch, and stuffed a dozen cookies into the pockets of her once-a-year ruffled dress.

The voice came again with another sharp tap on the door. "Do you remember me from church, Patricia?" Another sharp tap. "I helped you get a plate of barbecued beans last Easter?" A slow twist of the doorknob. "Is your dad or mom home, hon? Can I come in?"

The white-lady voice didn't sound like it was going to go away.

At first Patricia had tried to wash the dishes just in case Mom came back. After a couple of days, she stopped using dishes and opened cans one by one by one, eating with the same crusted spoon whatever she found inside, digging and scraping to the last bean, licking the sides as far as her tongue could reach, wiping her mouth on the unraveled skirt she'd worn since the second day everyone had gone away again and left her all alone.

"Can I come in, honey?"

Now only three cans of little oranges balanced themselves on the sticky counter, but she couldn't eat them because they were her mom's favorite. If her dad came home, he could fry potatoes with onions he chopped on the split cedar plank they used for a cutting board and scrape them into a pan sizzling with grease saved from when they last had bacon. If her mom came home, she might carry still-warm hamburgers from the restaurant up the street, greasy fries and ketchupy brown paper bags signifying the depth of her motherly love. If no one came home, Patricia would either have to eat the cold canned oranges after all or go ahead and unlock the door and let that white woman come inside.

For the next year or so, Mabel was just like a mother to Patricia. Or at least what Patricia and Mabel tried to imagine a mother would be. Mabel had brisked in the door, already rolling up her sleeves, and in minutes the counters sparkled, the refrigerator hummed, and a shopping list lay placid on the table. One pound of hamburger, four potatoes, two onions. One bar of Ivory hand soap. One plastic bottle of dish soap. One medium-size box of laundry soap. One tube of toothpaste. Washcloths.

Peppermint.

When a sober Young Tom finally crept in the doorway of Mabel's apartment a few weeks after the latest try with the gang, Patricia sat forward in the cozy floral armchair she'd been allowed to claim as her special place every night after she and Mabel cooked and ate a round dinner and washed and put away the matching patterned plates and saucers. Tom's scrubbed daddy-face and water-slicked hair pleased Patricia into a smile.

"Hi Daddy."

"Hi sugarpuss."

Young Tom had tried many times to visit in the past days and weeks, but Mabel would never let him come in when he was drunk. More than once when Tom had brought some friends—a few times, Patricia thought one voice in the clamor must be her Grandpa, Old Tom—Mabel had closed the door firmly against their slobbered pleading and telephoned the police. As if they sensed the call, the whole rowdy bunch bumped down the hall and out the heavy glass doors. While Mabel waited by the phone and afterward murmured to the officers at the front door, Patricia tiptoed to the window and watched her dad and grandpa and a posse of stragglers stagger down Capitol Avenue and squirm themselves into a car abandoned on untended property at the edge of the village upon which all the people who lived on this street could look down.

"I saw you and Grandpa." Every time Patricia looked out the window she pictured her dad crawling into the car with her grandpa, four dirty men, and three giggling girls.

"I'm not drinking anymore, Patricia. I'm sober now, honey." He perched on as little of the couch as he could manage without sliding edge-first off the cushion. Shiny stiff-pinch shoes flattened themselves on Mabel's smoothly waxed and rug-covered floor. Patricia tried to imagine her daddy's knobby toes squashed inside those black-creased shoes.

He always used to take his shoes off as soon as he got home from fishing. He'd bounce into the bathroom and they'd hear the splash of tubwater and Young Tom's pleasure moan and out he would come, feet sparkling and bare, and except for the bed slippers he tucked his contented feet into when he ran up the street for cigarettes or beer or hamburgers and sometimes peppermint candy, he stayed barefoot all the time until he was called again to a boat.

"Would you like some coffee, Thomas?" Mabel handed him a steaming ceramic cup and minced back to the kitchen. Patricia watched Tom suck the dark liquid. The kitchen noises Mabel made weren't as comforting now as they were when it was just the two of them and it was almost time for another round dinner.

"You're not supposed to drink coffee at night." Patricia pulled her new plaid skirt over her knees. "It keeps you awake."

Tom slow-motioned the cup onto the coffee table and patted the seat beside him. Patricia glanced into the kitchen and darted to her daddy's side. She hugged his shoulder and smelled his face. He tucked her into his arms. She felt him swallow a choke and hold his shaking breath. He buried his face on her pigtailed neck and gripped her like he was drowning and she was his only hope to reach for one more last ragged breath.

∦ ‖ ∦

One scrap of earth. A cabin upon it, ready to receive and hold the summer's wealth. The woman who contemplates the cabin and its surroundings has turned away from the desires that once flooded her reason. Now she considers her minor needs. Although the summer is over, she knows she must remain vigilant. Her relatives the bears and the wolves are eager to add one more layer to their stored fat, preparing for the coming cold just as she must do. The gardened border that invites sunlight will soon have scant purpose. The windows placed to allow in the daylight will only suggest the light, and that for only a short portion of the day. The inviting smells of the wet forest will soon be covered with the blanket of snow that keeps them safe and fresh and alive until the time comes for their rebirth. It's time now to stock more firewood than would seem to be needed. It's time now to collect and dry or smoke or jar the fish and berries and roots and greens of the land. Outside, the raven cries.

The earth yields reluctantly. The earth, like a patient grandmother, prefers to wait. She accumulates the fallen leaves and undone bones and blood and seeds and holds her every part for the rain to wash and cleanse. For the rain to make new. For the rain to make one.

Do you see the glacier above the clearing in the seam of the mountain that holds our town in the palm of its hand and waits suspended for the correct time to advance or to retreat? Be like that glacier.

Be patient like that glacier.

Wait for the appropriate moment before you make your move. In the meantime, conceal your inclinations behind a well-carved screen. Offer patience as resistance. Reaching your goal often begins with remaining still. Remaining receptive. When forces oppose, victory will be kind to the one who crafts herself like this earth and like that glacier, to the one whose power allows her to wait.

Take Raven. Although most people consider his actions impetuous, that trait is only one small part of his nature. A greater part of any strong nature is the capacity to wait. When Raven wanted the Box of Daylight, he didn't rush at once to be born. He waited in the water until the moment came to allow himself to be swallowed. When he entered the woman's belly, he didn't cause himself to be born at once. He waited until the appropriate moment had arrived, and then he was born. After his birth, he waited until the proper time had come before he began to cry for the Box of Daylight. These are the things that Raven did to achieve his goal.

More than history cries upon this coveted scrap of earth. More than aunties and grandmothers. More than Raven. The wolves and the bear do more than cry: they have patience, and they wait. They wait for the proper time to sleep, to wake, to consider. They wait for the proper time to listen to the words of a woman who has learned the value of calculation, who has learned the power of waiting. She covers the ground with her patience.

After the end of summer, after the summer's rush, when everything has been gathered and stored and collected against the coming winter, all we can do is wait. Count the firewood, ponder the weather, await the coming night. When we become still, we hear the life-filled forest and the life-filled ocean preparing themselves for the coming cold. Enough of summer's romance: hemlock and spruce now tuck their hands to their bellies. Clouds now mask the moon. Berry bushes, no longer charming, spend their attention on turning their last few fruits into seeds. Even the mosses have ceased their creeping for another year. They might take measure of their progress, but they know they will lose ground, vigor, life, before the time comes to press forward again. In the meantime, like Raven, they wait.

We don't know the seasons that passed while Raven waited in that woman's belly, but the chances are that fall time was breaking and winter was on its way. When else would Raven, napping inside a dark belly listening for sounds in a dark world, make himself comfortable and settle in for the long wait? Like his relative the brown bear, he could wake if he wanted, but when the days are growing shorter and we have time for a thoughtful choice, turning over for a longer nap is most often the wiser thing to do. Kicking a bit, grumbling, making the woman inside whose belly he rested experience sudden longings for winter foods like dried fish and berries suspended in seal grease and shrunken, crisp herring eggs rustling on tindered branches. The sudden longing for one more sip of clean cold water before it forms itself into ice.

⁜ ‖ ⁜

Now that the land is cleared and the foundation is set and the walls have risen to enclose us against the falling wind and the undone sky, it's time to carve the hemlock stump into a polished stool, the leftover plank into a suitable table, the abandoned moss into a comfortable bed. It's time to collect the last few remnants from our retreating gardens and prepare ourselves to wait.

Keeping ourselves warm as we wait for darkness to ascend begins with a worthwhile fire. Building a fire in a woodstove may sound easy enough, but people who aren't lucky are forced to rely on their skill. First comes the moss we've gathered, suitable in this dried stage for many purposes, most especially to start the fire that will warm us in the chill and keep us alive in the cold.

Years ago when I lived among the redwoods, in a tiny cabin in a place called Loma Mar for what seems now no more than an instant yet longer than even a lifetime, my mother and the sons who were with me lived in the main house, which a fire had almost destroyed some months before, a house that was once high-end but had been sold to the young man who was now in the long process of restoring and replacing the burnt charred beams, the gutted kitchen, the water-damaged floors. It seemed the only things in the now-bare house that dared to promise relief from the draft and the gloom were the newly installed windows and the stone fireplace that had survived the months with almost no sign of the catastrophic fire that had led to our camping in and around the now-cold building, its bare rafters providing running space for the dozens of mice that had taken over the shelter, its uneven floor offering no welcome, its haphazard plumbing and wiring warning and thrilling my meager attempts at making a home. But my mother liked the fireplace and she liked the fire, and she spent hours every day sitting on the fireplace stoop and tending the flames, adding twigs and branches and sometimes logs, no doubt dreaming of those days when she was young, when she was charged with the chore of helping to mind the cookstove flames or the smokehouse embers or the campfire blaze, those days when heat rose unbidden from her body and radiated into the sky and warmed the fire itself. Now, the scant flame from the few bits of kindling her grandchildren brought to her often failed to warm even the nearby air, and never warmed her bones.

Years later, a little woodstove sat in the corner of the mobile home I bought after we finally came back home to Juneau. It seemed that only parts of downtown and one or two places on the old road leading out to Auke Bay were as I remembered them. Everything else was new, had been built after northern oil made the state feel rich. This trailer park seven miles from downtown had not many years before been willows and hemlock, and black bear still nosed around on its streets, looking for their old trails.

I was happy enough to have raised myself enough out of poverty to have a trailer I could say I owned, although I still longed to live downtown, where I could catch glimpses of myself as a young girl holding my mother's hand along the sidewalks and stairs of so long ago. My mother now lived in a senior housing apartment right downtown and walked every day or so along the very street where she must also have glimpsed her own remembered shadows.

My mother joined the rest of the family—my sons, who tried with varying degrees of success to make their homes in Alaska, their partners, their children—in my aged mobile home for holiday dinners and for occasional birthdays, but she never made a move to tend the fire. Although she'd grown so lean she was now no more than brittle bone and thin cold flesh, she sat on the soft couch across the room from the fire, tucked into a bright new sweater, sneakered feet lifted onto a stool carried to the room only for her comfort, surrounded by new babies and those generations who loved her and whose passions the years had not yet cooled, and allowed herself to be warmed by no more than her memories and the inevitable regret of a life not fully lived.

⊹ ‖ ⊹

My mother got her wish to move to somewhere distant, somewhere else, anywhere not-here, along about the time my second child was born. No babysitting for her. Grandchildren were all well and good for infrequent holidays and for store-bought birthday presents packaged and taped and sent through the mail, but helping take care of them—cooking, cleaning, babysitting day in day out—held no charm for a woman bent on seeing even part of the rest of the world. She might not be able to pay for unfettered sightseeing on slow-moving cruise ships or fast-moving airplanes, but she could damn well put in for transfers to places farther and farther away until she ended up clear across the country in Washington, DC, calling every Sunday afternoon at 2 o'clock California time, right after she must have heated an early TV dinner in the kitchenette oven of her studio apartment. It was years before I realized it must also have been right before the daily six-pack of chilled beer she told herself and no one else that she drank only to help her sleep. Only to soothe her digestion. Only to smother her waylaid memories, to subdue her if-only regrets. Only to bury her stillborn dreams. Only to keep herself from walking up and down the concrete Eastern seaboard streets and alleys, searching high and low for the shadow of the memory of a man she had long ago thought might one day come to love her.

I searched high and low for the same man my mother searched for, and with the same purpose. Every man I met was a man who might love me, a man who would want me, a man who could cherish and protect and understand me. A man to mend my unfinished dreams, to repair my unmet hopes.

I never found that man, just as my mother never found him, but I made up for it by looking around every corner and under every rock. I found men who didn't mind telling me they loved me, possibly even believed it themselves, just as I always believed it for a while. Like my mother, I never learned how to love or be loved by a man. Like my mother, the shadow of that one unloving man came to define too much of my life.

I may have found men who could have loved me, but the image of an unlovable self clouded my eyes and in every case eventually prevented me from admitting the possibility of being loved. I doubted everything that might have made me believe I could be loved. But that didn't keep me from chasing the thrill of the chance of being loved, of being wanted, and for a few hours in some cases, a few days too often more, a few months, or a time or two even a few years, I convinced myself that if I believed that a man—any man—loved me, it meant that I was loved.

Occasionally I would see a license plate from Alaska or a renovated bus painted with the words Alaska or Bust, and a burning jealousy would consume me that anyone could be making their way to my home while I was still so far away from that hope. Or I would hear a man's voice hollering across the summer-melt river, calling for a dog named Kenai, and I would want to jump into the mad cool Yuba and swim across the rushing water and grab that man by the elastic waistband of his faded blue swim trunks and tell him take me back to Alaska. Take me home. Love me.

As the only child of an unmarried woman who escaped into cutthroat canasta and four-handed pinochle whenever she could gather friends and family around the kitchen table, smoking Pall Malls and joking and laughing at the inconstancy of the hands the generations had been dealt, and into magazines and books when no one else was in the place to keep her company but me, I learned early to ignore the vagaries of my own life and enter the clothbound worlds of little white girls who solved mysteries before dinner and tidied up their wholesome chores before their unchanging bedtimes. Although my grandmother always spoke the Tlingit language to friends and uttered those incomparable expressions and metaphors and curses throughout the day, she, like all the other realistic modern Tlingit men and women, saw the English-language writing on the wall and forbade my mother to speak Tlingit and taught me only a few phrases quickly forgotten as I was marched through classrooms of girls and boys who with scrubbed-clean fingernails pointed out my natural inferiority and with wrinkled noses reminded me that I was no more than a dirty little Indian girl from the village. Even the books I learned how to check out from the children's section of the library taught me that I would never be the clean little girl who knew how to solve a mystery with enough time left on the always reliable clock that parsed out everyone else's day to take a warm bubbly bath in a porcelain bathtub, skin lovingly smoothed with scented soap, wrapped softly in a fluffy clean towel, and carried to a fresh bed with cool sheets. Instead, I would always be the little girl left standing outside the master's door, my grandmother's language stuck in my throat, kept warm by my mother's silence, a book containing the master's words my only escape.

∗ ‖ ∗

Like most old people whose family home has been torn down with nothing built to replace it, my mother dreaded ever being sent to live at a nursing home. She was certain if that ever happened she would never come back out. St. Anne's, decrepit now, had once been the hospital for white people, the place where she had taken me for weekly penicillin injections. The white-people's doctor scribbled on his papers and stepped out to murmur in the hall while my mother and I sat silent in the cold unfriendly room, waiting for instructions.

I had recovered, we had both endured, we had both traveled and wandered so far from home. We had both thought for different reasons that we would never return, but now here we were back in our birthplace, she to surrender to a bed in St. Anne's hospital after emergency room visits and liquids and pills and machines failed to undo the harm that decades of Pall Malls had done, me to regret all the laughter we hadn't shared, all the words we hadn't spoken, all the secrets we should and should not have uncovered.

My mother sat semi-reclined and frowning, fiddling with the oxygen tube stuck under her nostrils, her weathered, bent hand wrapped in white binding under which a trailing tube fed to her the intravenous mush of concocted nutrition that someone had deemed the most suitable for her needs and her condition. The serving trays always sat virtually untouched. As she had done when I moved into her apartment to cook and clean, to prepare soft noodles, to arrange them on a tray with napkin and fork and all my concealed regrets, she would never look my way. After I called two or three times, after I placed myself on the window side of her bed, after my need to be seen finally outweighed her need not to see me, she would stop fiddling with the tubes under her nose and would brave me a wavering, loving smile. "I'm all right, dear," she would answer, her words breaking between short breaths.

She adjusted the oxygen tubes, seeming to reassure herself that she was indeed still breathing. She gazed at the rectangle view of grayed sky and unhopeful clouds through the rigid window. She confessed that sometimes she still got hungry for dryfish.

We all get hungry for dryfish. Images flooded my mind, days and evenings filled with the summer-dried treat that like love needs only to be sucked on, needs only to be made wet with saliva stored like salty memories waiting for the sharp quick bite that invites savor, the stinging taste lingering in dark bentwood thoughts: winter days in the kitchen of the old house, my grandmother feeding the stove, keeping the room warm, stirring and tasting and fussing, offering tastes, nibbles of meat, a spoon of broth, teaching me to love what came from her hand and to believe what came from her lips. Most of the time the stovepot contained meat from a simmering bone, sometimes potatoes, sometimes an onion.

Grandma told stories of history, family stories, stories of the animals that share their world. She told me what owls meant and what to do if I ever saw myself walking toward me on the street. She told me about women who cried in the forest and women who married bears and what happened to the children of women who had almost died giving them birth. She told me about the winter wind and the summer darkness and she taught me to dance and to sing and she tucked me in every night that she was home, and every day she told me never to cry. She taught me to love gristle and grease. She taught me to love the smell of white man's bread toasted at the hottest place on the top of the cast-iron cookstove. She showed me how to get things done. She showed me what it meant to be beautiful. She fed me.

My mother had never been much of a cook. She did her best to rotate a few special dishes when I was young, but as soon as I could pick up a pot, she stopped cooking except for the occasional stew. I swallowed the memory of steaming bowls on the bare table, of buttered rolls. Now it was canned goods in our colonized cupboard. No more halibut heads from the cold-storage dock. Now we paid for everything. And we were expected to swallow it all. We swallowed all of it, even when it made us gag to choke it down.

When my mother had finally come back for good from the tuberculosis hospital, it had seemed to my grade-school eyes that everyone in the old house was sick and everyone was drinking. It had started to be hard even to get fish off the docks. It was already hard to get deer. It was like being poor was the only thing anyone could do. No wonder everybody drank. My mother used to wear a mask when Grandma and

I came to see her as she looked out the second-floor window of the Indian hospital. I could never tell if she was smiling. As a child, I didn't realize that it wasn't her choice to wear that mask. I didn't know that they made her wear it so she wouldn't breathe on anyone. I didn't know that they made her stay upstairs so she wouldn't touch me.

The doctors and nurses made her wash everything she used so no one would get dirty from her. They wouldn't let her come close to anyone. They wouldn't let her hug anyone. She never touched anyone the whole time she was hospitalized. Even the doctor and nurses put rubber gloves on their hands and used the tips of their fingers to listen to the depth of her breath and the beat of her heart. None of them wanted to touch her. For the rest of her life, she lived with the memory of being someone that nobody wanted to touch.

My grandmother told me stories when we walked to see my mother in the hospital window. She told me about the woman crying in the forest. She told me never to go into the forest alone. She warned me about going into the forest at all, especially at night. She said there was a woman there who was crying and holding a baby and if I found her I could get a wish. But first I would have to take her baby away from her and wait and hold it. Even though my grandmother told me never to go into the forest by myself, especially at night, she always said that if I heard that woman crying, I could go into the forest and find good luck, but only if I remembered everything she said to do.

My grandmother liked to talk to me in Tlingit when she was cooking and when she was washing clothes in that old wringer-washer. When she wanted me she called *Saan kal yek't! Haagu!* and I came running. She taught me to count in Tlingit and called me by my Tlingit name. She made up a Tlingit song just for me and danced with me while she sang it. She called me a blonde Indian.

But my grandmother never let my mother say anything in Tlingit. My mother understood it, and she whispered it under her breath. My mother and most of her generation had been punished if they spoke Tlingit. But as a child, my mother had been punished even when she didn't say words in the forbidden language. It seemed to her that she was always punished for something anyway.

At the end of our visits, my mother would move her head once to each side as if to deny the disappointment she felt at the end of a long path that was not of her design, not what she had hoped, could not yet be the end. She would close her eyes and whisper the words from which she had always taken comfort and which now completed her life.

Your father was the only man I ever loved.

⸫ ‖ ⸫

Old Tom strolls along the beach, feeling hungry again. Since he sobered up, it's been like he's hungry all the time. Walking along, he happens to spot a seal. Part of its belly is ripped out, but otherwise it looks okay. He keeps his eye on that seal, which before he noticed its bloody belly had appeared to be resting on the rocks. It doesn't move as he steps closer and closer a little bit at a time. He tests the air for the smell of rotting flesh. None of that, either. After some investigation—throwing manageable rocks at it from a careful distance, calling to it from the edge of the sedge-brush, asking it to turn its head and look at him—he walks up and down the beach gathering driftwood here and there. Luckily the driftwood is dry.

Old Tom builds himself a fire in a protected button of a cove, feeding it with driftwood and the logs scattered in the brush that were waiting there for just this purpose. He gathers the nerve to approach the dead seal more closely. Its belly is indeed ripped open. Its eyes stare out toward the ocean where one can assume it has always been meant to live and where it wants always to direct its continuing gaze. The cut of its bright-red flesh calls back memories of fresh seal meat cooked by his mother at the fire, his laughing father holding her by the waist, everyone barely able to contain their appetites, already tasting the seared, mouth-watering promise of dark rich meat for their bowls.

Old Tom drags the seal into the hidden place where coals from his fire are beginning to collect. He scrapes the glowing coals into the cavity where the seal's belly used to be. Immediately Old Tom smells the cooking flesh. He is already enjoying the taste.

Normally everyone knows not to eat such things. Normally, people understand that very little nourishment resides in the scavenged wild reminders of lost memories. Normally, Old Tom would be sitting with everyone else at the soup kitchen, hoping for canned corned beef soup or Styrofoam-wrapped past-their-prime hamburgers from the fast food place up the street. But hunger for something real has made Old Tom act in what many would say is a manner beneath his station. He stirs the coals in the seal's open belly, and inside the cavity a nicely cooked rockfish presents itself to Old Tom. He helps himself to dinner on the beach, where he almost never finds much in the way of bounty, but where today he has caught himself a fish.

Mabel liked to iron the ruffles of her starchy aprons. Ironing pillowcases and aprons, folding them into stiff creases, patting their crisp-smelling folds into neat straightened stacks in precise closets, she reassured herself that Patricia would become lovely and loveable as soon as she learned to take pleasure in these womanly duties and learned to keep herself as clean as Mabel kept her linens. Mabel prayed for and strove toward that glorious day.

Patricia proved to be a stubborn project. It was clear to Mabel that Patricia didn't deliberately gag at Mabel's steamed brussels sprouts, her baked stuffed green peppers, her parmesan cheese creamed hominy. It was clear to Mabel that Patricia's below-grade reading comprehension level was not because she didn't labor over the words and pictures in the books her teachers sent home for extra practice. It was clear that Patricia's bitten dirty fingernails were not the only reason Patricia couldn't hold the squat pencil properly between whitened thumb and callused middle finger. It was all too clear that Patricia's abilities simply didn't prepare her to match the other girls in her grade-school class. Nevertheless, Mabel knew, Patricia was capable of living a wholesome productive life, and to Mabel she was her dear girl, the evidence of her good works, Mabel's rescued dearest girl.

Teaching Patricia the art of setting an attractive table and introducing her to useful products to hide any hint of perspiration and, in short time, any hint of the many other bodily functions that unsurprisingly visited Patricia quite a bit sooner than they had visited Mabel were distasteful but necessary responsibilities that Mabel would not shirk. She loved Patricia and wanted nothing more than to help her realize her best potential, perhaps as a secretary—for no one could deny that with Alaska statehood had come many opportunities for the Natives that wouldn't have been dreamt of just a few years ago—or as a practical nurse—now that the Indian hospital was in the process of being replaced by new and modern facilities, a sincere girl who knew how to keep things clean would easily find work—or perhaps as a dutiful wife to a nice Native man, perhaps even a Native businessman or politician, one who would be important to Native progress now that the settlement act had dislodged their claims and finally made them join corporations instead of those outdated clans that some of them—Patricia's grandfather Old Tom, for instance—still tried to talk about whenever they got drunk and sentimental. At any rate, Mabel would do her best to teach Patricia all the womanly arts, and while she was at it she'd make sure Patricia's daddy, Young Tom he liked to be called, improved his lot as well. She'd make sure he sobered up and stopped fraternizing with his father and that crowd, and she'd begin by reminding him that in the desire for a proper identity he ought rightly to change his name from Young Tom to Thomas.

When Thomas first presented himself at Mabel's front door he was still Young Tom as far as Mabel was concerned. She wanted to call the police right away. How had he made it into the building? She'd been complaining to the landlord about the faulty latch on that door for months. But since Patricia stood right behind her, clearly ready to toss open the door and heave herself into her daddy's arms regardless of his stink, Mabel knew she'd best stay between Patricia and a fast way out the door, and let the telephone call wait. Mabel quieted Patricia with a pointed finger to pursed lips, and they remained still until they heard Tom's shuffling and the dim sound of the building door shushing behind him. Mabel comforted Patricia.

"Your father is inebriated. We can't let him in when he's like that. Who knows what he might do," Mabel whispered, her back ramrodded against the door's knob, her eyes listening for danger, her heart thrilling.

"He won't hurt us," Patricia protested. "Well, he won't hurt me, anyway." She evaluated Mabel's appeal with a sixth-grade schoolgirl's methodical eye. "My Daddy loves me."

"I'm sure he does, Patricia." Mabel understood a young girl's need to believe that her father loved her. "But he's not in his right mind when he's drinking, is he? He can't come in when he's in a disgraceful state like that." She bent her head at the sounds of distant yelling, pale eyes squinted sideways. "Well, he's gone now." She patted Patricia's arm and guided her to the couch. "I'm sure he'll come back when he's in a more suitable condition."

Mabel found good reason to call the police a few days later when Tom showed up at the door yet again, it must be a dozen instances by now, but this time with what sounded like at least a half dozen others, one of them most likely his sordid father, whom Mabel had many times seen rolling on the street, stained and soiled, on his way to a heathen's hell with his unclean activities and ill-mannered shouting. She always crossed the street when she saw him, no matter that he was Patricia's grandfather. She certainly never intended to let him into her home, drunk or sober. With a stern threatening glare at Patricia, she dialed the number for the police. She noticed a smudge on the receiver, frowned at Patricia, and made a mental note to go over—yet again—the proper way to dust and clean. By the time the police arrived, the hall was quiet and Patricia was back at her favorite relaxation perch, looking out at the water and mountains of Douglas Island. No harm there.

✳ ‖ ✳

That old grandfather at the Nass River most likely walked his beloved grandson around that richly furnished house, but it does not appear to be part of history that he ever thought to walk the grandchild outside. Perhaps that is because there was no clear way out—after all, even Raven would eventually be forced to escape through the smokehole, not one of his favorite leavetakings, to be sure. But that old man could probably make a way out, should he desire to do so. It's more likely that he chose not to take Raven on a walk outside because it was dark. Not so with that other grandparent, that grandmother. At first, that grandmother seldom even walked her grandson around the house. Uproar and confusion shaped that grandchild's days, just as colonial trauma meant them to do. Some survive, scars and all. Some become the walking wounded in this cultural war. Some are made only of pain. All are treasured. All are cherished. All are loved.

That grandson and his mother had arrived late in the summer, and the length of their first stay lasted—or, more accurately, that grandmother lasted—until just after Christmas. Four months filled with days of her grandson waiting for hours to be allowed into the other bedroom, four months filled with other days of her grandson waiting for hours to be allowed out of the other room. Four months of her grandson tiptoeing down the narrow hall to tell his grandmother that he was hungry or he was bored or he was thirsty. Four months of that grandmother coming home to find the house empty except for spilled corn flakes on the kitchen floor, dried oatmeal and lumpy strawberry jam smeared on the cluttered counter, dishes and food scraps piled in both sinks. Sounds of grief and anger delivered to the telephone in a darkened room beyond a closed door, sounds of laughter and games cheering the emptiness between her and a closed door, four months of that grandmother rising in the morning with the hope of sending her grandson off to school with a packed lunch and instructions to be good and to study hard, of cooking meals for him on Friday evening that he wouldn't see until Sunday night or Monday afternoon, of taking him to the store in a vain search for something as precious as a Box of Daylight so he might, by unexpected good fortune, avoid his predictable future.

On Christmas Day that grandmother stood bewildered but unsurprised in the living room, where she had set up a decorated tree with wrapped presents underneath. The comforting aroma of a stuffed holiday turkey added to the warmth, the open-face woodstove crackled with soft flames against the wet snow piling thick in the driveway, while her grandson was once again hustled out the door by his mother without a hello or a goodbye. Those four months of unexplained silences and darkened rooms and wasted food and always changing plans to move and unshared plans to stay and fallen-through plans to leave, all that must have frustrated and grieved and sorely irked that grandmother's heart.

On the day after Christmas, that grandmother voiced her reluctant decision that their circumstances didn't appear to be working and they would have to start thinking about another place for them to live. That afternoon, her grandson and his mother stood in the driveway in the knee-deep snow, announcing to everyone who would listen that in spite of her so-called love and her so-called promises always to help, that grandmother had evicted them from her warm house onto the freezing sidewalk with no more than an hour's notice. By the next school day, her grandson was back, living with that grandmother while his mother stayed first at her own mother's house and after two weeks at a women's shelter. That grandson lived with that grandmother until the end of the school year, when he moved with his mother for the rest of the summer into a one-room apartment in a project for homeless families.

It seems clear that the grandmother must then have gone back to work entertaining tourists with descriptions of whales and glaciers. She must have spent the next weeks and months telling stories of bears who lived at the edge of the village and stories of grandchildren who wanted every precious treasure that their grandparents possessed. She must have spent her time telling a story of one old man who had thought he would be happy if he could keep daylight and starlight for himself, had believed it until he was visited by a grandchild who wanted nothing more than all his grandfather's treasure.

I might have been born without a father, a child of the beach, as some of the older ladies no doubt quickly reproached, out of wedlock, as the church preachers would have roundly judged, had my mother been disposed to sit in the pew and listen to their rebuke, but my mother was proud of her baby girl, and when my grandmother was home, cooking and cleaning and taking care of me, the baby she loved to call her first grandchild, she loved me as much as my mother did, and perhaps she loved me even more than that when she joined friends in the downtown bars and the cannery workers on the summer docks and bragged about her first grandchild. Everybody doted.

Only five or six years after I was born, my mother allowed herself to be forced to marry the youngest son of a local family, one associated by kinship ties dating back beyond memory—those old memories having been made dirty by new teachings and then wiped clean by new laws—but it only took a few weeks for her to realize her awful mistake and file for a divorce in the white man's court and to assume the far more respectable practice of marking "Divorced" in the many boxes that demanded to know her marital status, her race, her nationality, her age, her education. She was determined to provide for her child a life that featured warmed rooms and a filled icebox, butterfly-blue dresses from the Sears catalog and a wrought-iron miniature woodstove from the hardware store's toy window, books and magazines from Juneau Drug, money for movies and record players and woolen winter coats and paisley scarves for me to tie under my chin. To that end, my mother learned to type and file and organize papers according to the white man's alphabet, and she worked her way up from serving food in local restaurants and sliming fish in canneries to rag-mopping the halls of working-for-statehood lawyers to dusting the filing cabinets of territorial judges to finally, at long last, sitting at a desk that the prim, well-dressed first assistant to the second daily secretary of the principal attorney for one of the foremost men in the main committee of the constitutional convention said my mother could use in her new duties as helper to the junior file clerk. They were proud to hire an Alaska Native girl who knew how to file their important papers. My mother was proud to have a job helping white people advance their busy pursuits, a job that guaranteed a green-tinted paycheck that she could cash twice a month, on the fifteenth day and on the calendar's last day, a job where she only had to report for work promptly at 8 a.m. on weekdays, a job where she was never asked to work at night, never on weekends, and almost never past white people's dinnertime, which she had long ago learned was 6 p.m., according to their ever-present bald-faced clocks. Life was bound to be good from there on out.

The new job working for statehood allowed my mother finally to rent a real apartment on the second floor of a three-story building resting precariously on the side of the steep mountain, looking down on South Franklin Street, where once she had served coffee to a uniformed man, had smiled at the shine in his friendly eyes, had thrilled at his unhurried touch, had given to him brave smiles to fortify her skin-deep courage. Those days were gone. She had long ago begun telling herself to put away the hope that one day soon he would return. That he would disembark from a ferry boat or climb down the airport's metal stairs rolled up to the opened door of a PBY, which somehow she would be walking by, carrying out an important errand, dressed in fine clean fashionable clothes, and he would recognize her at once and she would recognize him, and he would ask immediately about his baby daughter, whom he would confess he'd been longing to see almost as much as he had been longing for her, and she would tell him, Your daughter's fine, she's healthy, she's doing well in school. She has your chin.

By the time statehood arrived, bringing with it the beginning of fanfare for all the white people and the end of a paycheck for her, my mother had tucked those hopes into a shadowed corner of her mind, weighed them down with worries and care for my grandmother who by then drank nonstop every day, weighed them down with rousing family games of cribbage and canasta, weighed them down with ambitions for her new job at the Juneau branch of the Bureau of Indian Affairs, where like everywhere else, white people ran the place and made all the decisions while she and others like her typed and filed and tried to scrub the floors clean of white people's footprints and empty the wastebaskets of the remains of white people's crumpled-up trash and help the white people forget their discarded intentions. Weighed her hopes down with the thought that she might move away, she might travel, she might rid herself of the memories and regrets that covered this place like the untrustworthy mist that daily blanketed their stolen inland waters. It had been a long time since she'd unpacked and embraced those derelict hopes to see that man again, again to hear his voice, ever again to feel that perhaps a man could love her.

THREE

Regret and the Forest
Are Patient Teachers

OUR MISSION TO WAGE LIFE requires us never to allow our ardor to be damped. Although daily we might feel as though we are beaten down, our responsibility commands us to keep our passion fresh and our zeal undimmed. Whether we speak of love or friendship or family or study or self, our enthusiasm for our endeavors must never decline. No matter that fatigue assails our strength, that languor threatens our vigor, that melancholy has diminished our spirit. If our ardor has been damped, we are not ready to face the battle. Life comes in its own proper time. We cannot predict our every challenge, but we can make ready by guarding our fervor. All wise people, all those who survive, are guided by this advice. Every good thing from which we can learn does not fail to recommend this rule.

Take Raven. Although forces meant to thwart his resolve came at him time and time again, his ardor for the chase was never damped. From the first moment that he heard of that old man in that secluded house that contained an answer to the darkness, he never allowed his resolve to waver; his ardor was never diminished.

What fervor must it have taken to remain in the cold flowing water of that little river for the time it took the old man's daughter finally to come to that certain bend in the stream? How much heat must have risen from his ardor when the even darker night and its barely discernable lengthening shadows chilled the waters bubbling around him? He must have relied upon his passion to warm him in the cold, to shield him from all doubt, to encourage him when uncertainty whispered from the dark water's darkened edge.

Finally inside the unreachable house, what zeal must have heated Raven when he approached those forbidden containers? The flames of his love, almost his obsession, must have risen high enough to equal those of the house's fire, of the flames beneath the smokehole exactly like another smokehole in he which he had already once been caught, that inevitable consequence brought about by the forces of his ardor. And as he struggled to free himself from that trap, as he held tight in his beak the promise of light for the world, how hot must have burned his undiminished passion, how hot his undamped ardor.

✢ ‖ ✢

My first glimpse of Juneau after I've been away for any amount of time always quenches an ever-present thirst. I've seen Juneau from many directions and from many altitudes, in many kinds of weather, from near the top of the mountain overlooking the long wide view up the coast toward Klukwan and down the coast toward Sumdum, from the windows of jets and the windows of single-engine floatplanes, from the forward deck of a midsize cruise ship returning for a day filled with the business of turnaround, and from the front windshield of a borrowed ride into town to check the mail. From all these directions and altitudes, the sight of Juneau tucked at the foot of two mountains has never failed to provide me comfort, has never failed to seem to be opening her arms to receive me in her embrace, has never failed to soothe and reassure me with the welcome emanating from her soil, from her mountains, from her shoreline, from the ground where my mother's ashes rest next to my grandmother's ashes, which rest next to my grandmother's mother's remains, which all find rest not far from the place where my own ashes will be buried, ready to join the memory of my voice to the many calls welcoming the generations back home from any journey.

Traveling back home on the state ferry after twenty-five years of passive exile in California, I disembarked at Ketchikan, the first Alaska port of call, where I lived for two years. From time to time during those two years, I visited the village of Saxman and for the first time saw the stunning collection of totem poles housed there. Among the most striking of the poles was a memorial pole depicting a young man with his arm caught by a giant clam.

These visits took place in the late 1980s, before the commercial development of Saxman village, and there were no tour guides or visitors' tents showing videos and explaining the history of the people original to this part of the land. But there were friendly residents who were willing to talk about the poles and about their meaning, and on one sunny day lounging on the grass, surrounded by carved poles, listening to my distant relatives laugh and tell stories, I first learned about that young man whose arm was caught by a giant clam, who lost his life, who was mourned and remembered and memorialized in story and in carved pole as a cautionary lesson to those who would reach into traps.

People say that when Tlingit emissaries first talked to white men, they were offered food and other enticements. It's said that when they first looked at the white man's rice, they thought that they were being offered maggots. When white men first gave them fermented wine or bottled rum, Tlingit traders must have thought it a supernatural drink that made them see the world in a different and meaningful way. When adventurous Tlingit children tasted their first spoonfuls of sugar, they must have thought it was much too sweet for their mouths.

Who knows what made that young man reach his arm into the clutches of a giant clam? Perhaps it was curiosity. Perhaps he imagined hidden riches and secret prizes. Perhaps he was simply hungry. Perhaps he supposed he could cut the flesh of the giant shellfish and feed his family, even the whole village, for a week or for a month. Perhaps it was only greed. No matter the reason, he could not have understood the danger. For the risk was not merely the threat of that giant hardened shell closing around his impetuous arm, something he might have thought would at most cause a tender bruise, a grip that he could sooner or later escape. The greater risk, the risk he did not have sufficient time to avoid, came from the inexorable tide.

The mystery of an unknown prize is surely part of its appeal. In my own life, I've often reached for unfamiliar treasure. I've sometimes been willing to risk my safety for a chance at improbable wealth, most often the imagined richness that comes with being wanted. Sometimes my daring was rewarded. Sometimes the maggots in my life turned out to be delicious rice. Yet good fortune is seldom the case. Most often, the alcoholic cup diminishes our spirit and threatens to lay its curse upon our generations. Far more frequently, the offered spoon of sugar rots our teeth. Far more frequently, we are raised to speak a language that is new to our grandparents, and we cannot easily find the words that overcome the space between us and our own generations.

Most often, attending new churches made me forget the spirituality and worldview revealed to me in my grandmother's stories and descriptions of our place. Too often, when I learned someone else's history, someone else's heroes, someone else's truths, I forgot my own. Too often I clamored for dividends, demanding that my pitiful corporation mine and log our beloved land so I could reach into unknown places and pull out empty trinkets.

Whether from curiosity, hunger, or greed, or because we had no choice, everyone has reached blindly into the unknown. Now we are all caught in the grip of a giant trap, and now the tide has come upon us.

But we can still daily take wisdom from the story of the man who was caught in a deathly grip and because of it lost his life. We can still pause to consider our choices. We can still be mindful of what has become of our own culture, and we can love what remains of our land. We can remember our own stories. We can now reach not into a trap but into the box of wisdom. With patience, we can remember who we are. With patience, we can transform the tide.

We seek reason for discomfort and confusion. We press meaning from haphazard events, assign purpose to the random lifting of one packed box, to the accidental turn that set our years on unplanned paths. But discomfort can hardly be called suffering, and every time we try to feel sorry for ourselves we cannot ignore the images of the many people who have undergone real suffering, oftentimes with little purpose and always for no good reason. Much of the time, though, our intellectual search for meaning is fleeting, and after a moment or two of wondering, we get back to the business of measuring our own pain.

✦ ‖ ✦

On the day Tom's sober knock finally sounded on the door, Mabel unfastened the latch, twisted the lock, and cracked the door as far as the safety chain allowed. "Yes?" she said in her most cultured voice.

Patricia crowded behind her, much closer than Mabel could ever get her in even the most tasteful hug.

"How are you feeling today, Thomas?" Mabel asked.

Young Tom, clean-shaven, dressed in store-bought chinos and a crisp button-up shirt, clearly uneasy but just as clearly determined, nodded his head. "Hello, Miss Mabel. I'm here to see my daughter."

"Of course, Thomas," Mabel smiled. She closed the door to undo the chain and allow him into her home. She wanted him to understand that she believed he could become an acceptable man, a suitable father, a credit not only to his people but to society as well. She wanted him to know that she was willing and able to help him do just that. "Please sit down."

She guided him with a brush of her hand through the newly freshened air, gesturing toward her flowered chintz sofa. "Would you like some coffee?"

Despite Mabel's frown, Patricia hurled herself at her father. She grabbed his sleeved elbow and wrapped her knees around his shaky legs. Mabel was pleased to see that Thomas couldn't help a grin. She turned toward the railcar kitchen and pretended not to listen to their conversation as she heated tea for herself and Patricia, a special treat today, and poured coffee for Thomas. She folded three yellow cloth napkins—kept for company and what was Thomas if not company?—but decided against the gilt-bordered teacup and matching saucer for him, choosing instead a ceramic cup much like the ones used down at the sleazy café all the Natives and other alcoholics frequented. She poured steaming water into two cups and hot black liquid into the mug, placed sugar and cream onto the serving tray, and set it on the coffee table in front of Thomas and Patricia, who now snuggled next to one another in a dear embrace. Mabel's heart warmed at the tender sight.

"Here, dear," she exclaimed to a disconcerted Patricia. "I've made tea for you as a special treat." She dipped the peppermint teabag into the cup. "One lump or two, dear?"

Patricia sat quiet, holding onto her dad.

"One lump or two, Patricia?" Mabel repeated.

"Huh?" Patricia glanced at her father, but he was concentrating on examining the scab of a scratch on his thumb and seemed not to notice the question.

"One lump or two, Patricia?" Mabel waited another moment. "Patricia, how many sugars do you want in your tea?"

"Oh!" Patricia's face cleared. "Seven, please." The girl held her cup toward Mabel's offer of two lumps of sugar held in dainty tongs above the tray.

"Two will do, Patricia. Ladies don't put seven cubes of sugar in their tea." She dropped two cubes into Patricia's disappointed tea.

"Oh." Patricia stirred the sugar into her tea. She dipped the teabag in and out of the thin cup. She balanced the saucer on her knee, pushed up against the cold sharp edge of Mabel's stern hospitality.

"Sit back, Thomas!" Mabel twinkled. "Here's your coffee. Make yourself comfortable!" She pushed the tray a little closer. When he didn't move, she handed him the steaming cup. "One lump or two, Thomas?" She positioned the sugar bowl back in its place next to the cream when he shook his head at her offer. She pointed her chin at the girl. "Patricia, why don't you sit over there so you can drink your tea and your father can have some coffee."

Patricia unwound herself from her father and settled herself in the chair where Mabel wanted her. They emptied their cups in silence.

Mabel carried the tray back to the kitchen. When she turned to join them in the living room, Patricia was back at her father's side, Tom's face buried in his daughter's pigtails, unable to hide his trembling.

⊹ ‖ ⊹

The land has been cleared, the foundation is set, walls have risen to protect me against the growing winds. I've collected the last few remnants from the now-thin gardens. I am now prepared to wait. I've started a worthwhile fire with moss

I have gathered and dried against the approaching season. I've stocked branches and driftwood and logs and stumps in a ready place next to my cabin, positioned on this little scrap of earth to which I will always belong. On the still-faint flame I arrange a few twigs, another fluff of moss, a handful of small branches. I breathe fervor into the flame's promise. Here I nurture the beginning of a blaze that will keep me alive throughout the coming cold, a blaze to warm my cold bones as I await my next release into the light.

Every winter morning finds me scattering food to the ravens. During the summer I've saved fish scraps and bones, stuffing them into cans and bags and tucking them in a corner of the freezer against these snow-covered days. During the fall I've folded dried bags of days-old bread and stiff leftover pancakes into the crook of the pantry's shelf, occasionally checking the grease-stained wrap and adding another day's crumbs to its wrinkled promise. Now I pick out bones from last night's meal, examine fresh bread for one stale slice, weigh the worth of an unopened pack of uncrumbled saltines against my relatives' harsh hunger. As I clear a path through the snow, past the whisper of last summer's garden, past the now-silent brook, I drop bits of biscuit behind me like a child searching for a gingerbread oven in which to push a fattened witch. My raven relatives unfailingly pick away my safe path home and consign me to sweet fate, fluttering their panicked wings if I turn my face in the direction of their vigilant regard.

Down to the beach to view the day. Measure the snow-cover on the distant mountains. Listen for sounds in the forest. Breathe the cold. Collect one or two pieces of driftwood to dry in front of the fire, to warm me in my cabin. Turn away from the wind and freezing rain exciting the waters near the shore, back to the scrap of earth upon which I have built my home. As I enter the day, as I enter the light, as I approach the idea of home, wind and rain change to gentle snow. I hurry into comfort.

My grandmother's name was Saawdu.oo. Ruth Willard Hayes. She chopped wood for the cookstove and washed clothes with a scrub-board. She rolled a scarf around her head, picked up a knife, and went to work sliming fish. After putting me to sleep, she bathed herself, and the next day she powdered her face while I watched. She drew eyebrows atop brilliant knowing eyes and reminded me from my first day: Get ready. Be prepared. Don't let anything surprise you. You must be willing to face every threat.

For the first few years of my life, I lived with Saawdu.oo while my mother was in the hospital for tuberculosis. During those years, my grandmother taught me how to see the world. She taught me to listen to the spiders in our house, for they knew the things that I needed to know.

During summers, I sat on the hill behind our old house and waited for her to call me in for soup or to send me on a chore. During fall, I tried not to go to school. Spring was not much different from winter. In winter, I listened for the grandfather about whom my grandmother told me, the Taku wind, and hoped for a sled to ride down frozen Capitol Avenue. Inside the house, I stayed away from the snow that drifted under the door into the dark hall. I sat in the kitchen and with my grandmother waited for my grandfather to come home. We both wondered what mood he would bring with him through the door with the drifted snow. With the wind. With a wide smile carrying gifts or with a cold grip on a cheap bottle of something to help him forget.

Winter in Lingit Aani brings magpies and ravens. Eagles allow themselves to be more freely seen. We take measure of the wood, we sweep the stove, we unpack blankets from their summer store. We watch the mountains and the birds for marks of early snow. We wait.

Unlike spring, winter does not bring signs of spiders into the house. Like the bears, they must be holing up somewhere. Or dying. Or dead.

My grandmother instructed me about spiders. Don't hurt them, she warned. Learn from them. Watch them. Learn.

Spiders hunt. Although we might consider them bashful around humans, they show no such timid spirit with their prey. Even the webspinners remain at the ready, testing their woven silk for the struggles of unwary victims. Though their size is small, their nature persuades us to boldness.

Spiders greet the world early. They wake and get busy early in the day and early in the spring. While the more familiar admonition for those of us who would lead a correct life is to wake before the ravens, rising before the spiders behooves us even more. The industry of spiders exemplifies right living.

In the garden, spiders occasionally mimic the colors of nearby blooms. Their sly lurking reminds us that boldness and industry, without which we cannot prevail, suffer in the absence of cunning.

When still a newly married young woman, my grandmother traveled to Klukwan to visit her dying sister and retrieve the youngest child, a fresh-born girl named Kaaxkwei. With the child, she and her new husband, Ernie, traveled back to Juneau. In two or three years, her first natural child was born. She eventually gave birth to three boys and two girls. One baby boy died. She and Ernie began to drink.

Spiders are persistent. One sleepy morning years after I had begun teaching my own grandchildren about spiders, as I waited for warm water from the faucet in the hand sink, I glimpsed a spider whirling down the drain. I washed my hands at another sink and told myself there was nothing I could have done. I promised myself and the spider that from now on I would more carefully attend to the presence of other lives.

Normally I trap spiders in a clean glass jar, blocking their escape with a stiff paper forced at the feet of their panic, and release them onto the wet ground outside the front door. I send them all away with my good wishes. Now, I mourned my role in one spider's death. I imagined its headlong rush into the dark churning void. But what could I have done? I asked myself in hopes of absolution. My grandmother's words held no room for pardon: I could have been precise. I could have watched. I could have been mindful.

Hours later, I braved the hand basin again just in time to witness that spider summiting the drain's final climb. Without a moment for rest, she began again her labor to overcome the sink's smooth walls. While I retrieved a sparkled glass and picked through recent cardboard, I thanked her for the lesson. She had reminded me to persevere.

My grandmother's oldest child, the baby girl she'd retrieved from Klukwan, grew into a good worker. She worked at the café and in the hospital. She got pregnant. She remained unmarried and gave birth to a baby girl. My grandmother disapproved. But the grown daughter did a lot of work around the house and paid a lot of the bills and bought a lot of groceries, so my grandmother could only yell, scold, and wait for my grandfather to come home drunk or sober. The grown daughter got tuberculosis and was sent into the hospital. My grandmother fit the new baby into her life.

Spiders exhibit qualities to which I can only aspire. Patience. Determination. Common sense. I don't know what my grandmother meant for me to learn when she taught me not to disturb the spiders I discovered crawling along our walls or scurrying into corners. But I know that by teaching me to respect this one small creature's life, she taught me reverence for every living thing. By cautioning me to listen to spiders, she taught me to listen to the world.

I don't flatter myself that my own grandchildren, now grown with families of their own but not yet exempt from my instruction, pay any more attention to my admonitions than I did to my own grandmother's lectures. But I do believe that one day they will remember me as I remember her: teaching me in a voice of scolding grandmotherly love, ready to dance with me, ready to answer any question. Ready to watch with silent wisdom while I listen for the whispers of others.

After the oldest daughter came home from the hospital, after all the children were grown or dead, after everyone had finally moved out and my grandmother found herself alone in the old house, she and her new man rented an apartment closer to town and drank most of the time. He often raised his hand to her. She wrapped herself up in a knee-length coat and covered her face. When a young girl ran into the ground-floor apartment to visit her grandmother, he held back his raised arm and turned away.

She shapes her web. She drops herself with utmost faith into the abyss. She and her sisters hang themselves from the ceiling here and there. They focus themselves against the light. I sweep the hint of their shadows from my cheek. I come across them on the walls and find them crawling in slippery circles in the tub, unmindful of the coming flood. I retrieve a sparkled empty glass and pick through recent papers for stiff board. She senses me and tries to flee, but where can we run when we're trapped by porcelain walls?

When her oldest daughter—the one she had retrieved from Klukwan, the one who didn't know she wasn't her mother's natural child until one thoughtless moment when the knowledge was thrown at her across a room, across a fracture, across a broken life—left the state vowing never to return, my grandmother carried on with the rest of her life. Until one cold day in the midst of a Taku wind, when she walked south on South Franklin Street instead of in the northern direction that would have led her quickly home. Two weeks later, her oldest daughter forced her eyes to read the unwanted words in the unwelcome letter from a younger sister telling her of her mother's lonely death. Found on the ground in the cold winter. Found wrapped in a knee-length coat. Found alone.

She shapes her web, spinning one line, drops herself into the unknown, is swept unmindfully from unseeing faces, finds the smooth destination, slips repeatedly from smooth unforgiving walls, is flooded into the dark, clinging by desperation alone against the circle's side. When at last the flood ends she climbs toward the light, only to be caught beneath the transparent glass and forced upon the cardboard, carried into the cold, dropped without ceremony onto the pebbles, the clover, the dirt. She overcomes every danger. She allows nothing to surprise her. As my grandmother always knew, we must be like the spider from our first day to our last. We must be willing to face every threat.

✢ ▍ ✢

We pride ourselves on being able to withstand pain until we realize we have never experienced pain. Whether a twisted or broken ankle, a headache, a minor burn, we allow ourselves to believe that we have met those debilities with resolute strength. A twisted or broken heart, a fleeting despair, a minor disgrace, we meet those burdens with commendable aplomb. We somehow learn to live even with major grief, with the pain that accompanies the knowledge that the physical world has been made a lesser place by the sudden absence of one more person who has loved us all our lives. With the challenges of such experiences, with the reassurance that we know how to grit our teeth and endure, we allow ourselves and those around us to think we can withstand any pain.

To withstand a growing pain, the kind that makes a person dread each move, each urge, each desire, calls for more than patience and resolve. It calls for directed passion. When the years that have seen us gripped by physical and emotional ardor have long since passed, we miss them not at all. Now and then, when we are reminded of the times we were willing to climb mountains, cross rivers, dance all night, study all day, work three jobs, take care of children, cook, clean, and keep an eye out for unclaimed men, we may wonder at our placid acceptance of the absence of those urges. But we find a deeper passion, a more persistent ardor, in the desire to remain constant for sons and daughters and grandchildren, to nurture the urge to weave words into stories, to help the people who come our way negotiate the achingly familiar perils along the rocky coasts of their own youth. We find that ardor isn't brief, passion isn't momentary, ardor cannot be thin. When passion is full-grown, it brings with it the knowledge that our ardor must be persistent. When passion is full-grown, it brings with it the steadfast resolve to see the challenge through.

Chilkat weaving, the complex art of making woven blankets out of mountain goat hair, cedar bark, natural dyes, and stylized vision, the threads hanging from racks, the weavers following pattern boards painted with designs that reveal only half the fullness of varied shapes, the other halves their mirrored opposites, painted images replicated in knotted threads and braided yellows and raveled black, symbolizes the intricate sophistication of Northwest Coast blanket-weavers.

My mother's Auntie Jennie was a Chilkat weaver, but I am not.

Spruce root basketry, young, tough, spring trailings tightly pulled together to hold seal oil, cooking water, tasty berries, or loosely woven to hold fresh clams, branches, children's playthings, manifests an ancient human understanding that blends stunning art and daily life persuaded to breath by the touch of basket-weavers. My family once owned baskets woven from spruce root by the hands of basket-weaving artists, relatives who could admit to such accomplishments with suitable modesty and pride, but I cannot.

Deft flesh-weavers wield sharpest knives, slice thin and not-so-thin sheets of red salmon almost still wriggling, longing always to strive upstream, and they set that salmon flesh to hang and bathe in softly stinging woodsmoke faded into the thickened air, those same flesh-weavers watching and touching and smelling and feeling and tasting and pressing and chewing and taking down the dried sheets one by one by one, trying not to show pride in this, the finest batch of woven flesh that, when winter comes and it's time for mourning followed by laughter, old men will desire and young women will covet. Men and women take up their careful summer knives and with purpose weave from the generous flesh of salmon and halibut the coming winter's sustenance to delight the mouths of babes and old ones. But I do not.

They weave from the land and the sea the devil's club salve, the Hudson Bay tea, the dried black seaweed, the smoked clams and cockles, the berry medleys, the jars of seal oil, the many rich splendor-filled tastes and comforts and warmth offered by this loving place. But I do not. I can only weave weak threads made from poor words in an imitated language to form a thin blanket, an insufficient basket, an unsatisfying meal that can only suppose what must have been, can only suggest what might still be.

Take Raven. When he had been stuck before in that other smokehole, the smoldering fire turning his feathers from the pale washed-out covering with which he had fooled that old man to the color of darkening smoke, darker smoke, darkened smoke, he didn't give up. He kept struggling. He did not allow his ardor to be dampened.

Ever since I first heard about the change of Raven's feathers, I wondered what it could mean. When I first heard that in one of Raven's early manifestations, he presented himself as a white bird, it was unclear to me how such a thing could be. Rumors likening his feathers to the sails of the first sighting of an off-course ship generations ago couldn't be the whole story, I assured myself. I could form an image of people wondering at a craft the size of twenty war canoes top to bottom and a whole hand's silhouette from front to back, gesturing to its approach with fingers trembling, with hands uncertain whether to grab weapons or to cover the unbelieving widening eyes blinking in the ship's direction. Even though the ship must have been a good distance away, the first people to see it must have been knocked back a step or two by their astonishment.

Old stories of Raven before he was black, of his wings as wide as a hand's worth of war canoes, of Raven with feathers the color of fresh snow, the color of the clean hard-packed unbroken ice that covers the most desperate paths over the mountains that surround and protect us and hold our towns in the palms of their own hands and seek the shoreline that these first people to see this sight then faced, marveling and wondering at the coming of something even the most vivid of their nightmares could never have conjured—none of those old stories could have been enough to prepare these unbelieving people for a sight as astonishing, as out of place, as incongruent, as those men and women dressed as Raven appearing to them offshore, oversized and unexpected, clothed in white, bringing with them never-before-seen gifts made of fire and maggots.

✦ ‖ ✦

That old man in that old house at the top of the Nass River must finally have come to a day when he could do no other than realize that his beloved grandson had betrayed his precious love. So it was that the grandmother also came to a day when she could do no other than admit that her own grandson had done the same, had stolen her box of treasured jewelry and that the place where she kept those carved bracelets she meant one day to give to him was now as empty as that money jar had been those years before.

The years had uncovered for her a path lined by disappointment and deception, heartbreak, failure, and defeat. Those colonial consequences, those symptoms of intergenerational trauma, those sighs of resignation, had visited her house, her family, her neighborhood, her sight. That grandmother had given to her own grandchild the lessons her grandmother had given to her, lessons each grandmother had received from the grandmother before her. Those lessons, this grandmother now willed herself to believe, would prevail against the suicide rates and dropout statistics, the alcohol and loss, sickness and miseries, incarcerations and anger, the depression, the despair. If we listen to the generations, that grandmother had to believe, we will hear them tell us to remember who we are, to remember what we have come through, to go forward even when it seems as though a grandchild has stolen all the light and has taken all the treasure from our life.

⋇ ∥ ⋇

Old Tom wanders along the beach. He's thinking about the party he'd heard about just that morning at the Glory Hole food line. A wedding celebration, they said. For an old friend from Sitka, it turns out.

Old Tom cleans himself up with fresh water from his favorite little drip of a waterfall just over from his favorite button of a cove. He arranges his hair with the comb he carries in his back pocket. He heads back downtown, walking on South Franklin Street northward toward the Baranof Hotel, past the docks where the cold-storage castoffs once offered all you can eat and fishing boats once tied up, but where now only cruise ships and their cargo of money transmitted through the complacent pockets of middle-class tourists could be seen in the summer, and in the winter, only long-dead ghosts and the temptations of slippery death.

Along the way to the street where he has heard there will be a party, Old Tom happens upon a liquor store. The very one to which he used to sneak for wine in the days when he slept and drank and sang in the abandoned car on the property in the village. The very one that watched him like a hungry eagle when he slipped in the door on the alcohol side of the store. The very one. Now, though, the clerks don't pay him as much attention as they did when he used to drink. Now, instead of watching him like a drunk Indian, they just watch him like an Indian. Old Tom congratulates himself for the substantial progress he has made in this white man's sharp-eyed world.

Old Tom chooses a package of dried noodles, chicken variety. He can almost smell them now. As soon as they're cooked, the noodles will begin to soak and swell in the salty MSG-flavored broth, so the whole package is meant to be eaten at the same serving. For that reason, Old Tom rarely cooks them. Because he's hungry all the time, he likes to eat slow. But today he decides to treat himself to these chicken-flavored noodles.

On the curb just after he crosses the street and is about to enter the village, Old Tom kneels to tuck the noodles into his suddenly heavy backpack. Look at that, he tells himself. In the stiff backpack, perched above his still damp comb, he finds four bottles of Lancers wine. He finds them. Yes, he finds them right there in his stiff backpack. They must have jumped in there while the clerk wasn't watching. What good luck. Now he won't be empty-handed. He can carry these bottles of cheer to the party. He's sober now, but he has nothing against other people searching everywhere to see if they can find a taste of comfort and joy.

Old Tom walks toward the laughter and happy-cries in one of the last openly occupied houses in the old village. He walks toward smiles and ripe lust, toward someone's idea of a future. At the party, he congratulates his smitten friend and stands up to the new wife's pregnant frown. Old Tom makes a joke about tonight. He smells the laughter. He feels the second-hand lust.

Someone asks for another glass of wine. Old Tom's newly married friend rummages around in the kitchen and in plain brown-paper bags in the living room, but it's clear that there's just soda and water left. There's no more wine! the groom cries. I'm embarrassed to say it's all gone!

Old Tom opens his stiff pack and pulls out his four bottles of Lancers. Here! he calls to his friend. Let's open these bottles! Let's drink!

After that day, all the friends who were at the party remark that Old Tom's newly married friend had served Tokay at the start and had saved the better wine for last. After that day, all the friends who were at the party and all the people who heard that story of the miracle cast suspicious, hopeful eyes at Old Tom. After that day, they wonder at the treasures that must be hidden inside Old Tom's ragged bundle.

Mabel decided to allow Thomas into her bed after the first time he'd been sober for six months in a row. He'd stopped that pointless commercial fishing, which even when it paid was a grease spot on the road to hell and when it didn't pay was nothing more than an excuse to horseplay with the rest of the crew, leave town for weeks at a time, and then come back sun-worn, salt-parched, and slam-out tired. To set him on the righteous road to sober redemption, Mabel arranged for him to pack groceries and retrieve carts for the food market down the street in exchange for a respectable hourly wage. At first she insisted that he look for an apartment he could afford on his own, but it quickly came to her that the Lord's work would more efficiently be done if she kept a closer eye on him and on his paycheck.

He'd been sober for a few weeks and was coming to dinner every day after his shift at the store. At the beginning, he'd take his leave at Patricia's bedtime, headed for the makeshift room he was renting from the pastor, walls of boxes constructing three sides of a precarious room on one side of the church basement. He met the pastor every evening at 9 o'clock to be let in the outside door to the just-below-ground-level basement, where the pastor would walk in before him and test the locks on the door that led upstairs. Tom would pick his way to his designated corner, the pastor would leave, and Tom would rest on his cot in the lamplit, darkened room, pale summer daylight still visible through the high windows, the occasional glimpse of a distant winged seagull reminding Tom of boisterous laughter and mended fishing nets and the hope of a good summer catch. When at last he closed his eyes, he shot headlong down a dark, narrow tunnel on the wheels of an empty cart, alone and afraid, not even the haphazard sounds of wandering voices enough to light his way to any sort of comfort.

"How is your room working out, Thomas?" Mabel asked one evening after dinner had been cleared, dishes washed, crumbs swept away, tablecloth folded, washed dishes dried, chairs pushed in, napkins inspected, dried dishes placed in cupboards, dining table polished. The possibility of taking after-dinner pleasure in the memory of food well served sank into Young Tom's belly and remained there, held down like an aching, unfulfilled belch. Patricia sat quiet at the square kitchen table, ruled paper and sharp-cornered books spread across the crisp gingham tablecloth, pencil in hand. Tom thought his daughter seemed to be studying and eavesdropping at the same time.

"I sleep," Tom replied. "I'm usually awake before the pastor lets himself in and kicks me out at nine."

"Well, I'm sure he's not actually kicking you out, Thomas.

He just wants to satisfy himself that you're doing well." Mabel crossed her nyloned legs. "Today's your payday and your rent would be due tomorrow if you still want to stay there. Do you want to keep staying there, Thomas?"

Tom wasn't staying on an old cot constructed out of bedsprings and back pain because he liked it, checking in and out just like jail but without the company, bumping into the flimsy cardboard walls two or three times a week, balancing the boxes back into a makeshift wall before the pastor showed up to lock him in or lock him out. He wasn't doing any of that because he liked it.

He'd been surprised the first time he'd knocked into the wall and spilled empty boxes across the floor. For some reason he'd thought they contained useful things, or at least something that had weight. For some reason, he'd thought that the walls constructed to keep him in and keep him out possessed a useful purpose. For some reason, he'd thought that the walls that made his prison were anything but empty.

"I didn't think I had a choice whether I stayed there or not," Tom said. "I thought that was what I had to do so I could keep seeing my daughter."

"I wouldn't necessarily put it that way, Thomas," Mabel said.

"How is it, then? If I move out of there can I still come see Patricia?"

"Of course! But you know we all agree that you have to stay in a location suitable for sobriety, one that doesn't present temptation, a place where you can keep clean and report for work on time and eat a balanced diet."

Tom stayed quiet.

❖ ❘❘ ❖

We live in shadows. We live in the shadows of women who if they were features of landscape would be the tallest mountains, the widest rivers, the deepest part of our literary oceans, while we cling to narrow shores. While we wade in ankle-deep shoals. While we bluster at barnacles. We live in the shadows of men whose words paint the wings of the brightest songbirds and echo the most lyrical rustlings of the forest. We haunt the near borders, listening, hoping one day to understand, to hear their message, to believe. We imagine ourselves swimming out beyond safety into the deepest waters.

We are here to become one another: all our lives we have been forced to study and practice how to be someone else, and all our lives those others have imagined themselves as us. We live in each other's shadows.

I was taught by my Tlingit grandmother to see the world through an Indigenous lens. As a student in the years that followed, I was taught to see the world through a colonial lens. As the only child of a single mother who loved to read, I learned at an early age the pleasures of imagined escape through the page into another world. As the first grandchild of a no-nonsense woman who perceived the world in the old way, I listened to her stories and learned to recognize that everything is alive and everything is connected.

My mother drank Hills Brothers coffee. She smoked Pall Malls. She shuffled worn blue cards and dealt Bicycle hands of pinochle and canasta, poured herself a cuppa steaming joe, flashed an etched Zippo with a quick snap—the one bit of her memory she let me see—the one remnant of her memory from which I built an imagined ghost to call my father.

She planned budgeted orders from Sears and Montgomery Ward catalogs: two pleated skirts, three pastel blouses, four pair of pink-laced anklets. No shoes this year, no winter coat, no beads, no feathers, no history. We shopped for mail-order acceptance following send-away instructions. We searched for our mislaid culture in shelved boxes of pilot bread. Sailor Boy, Tang, Libby's corned beef—traditional foods of our colonized cupboard.

Someone is living my life. Someone knows my song. Someone casts a shadow as I sit here dreaming that I write. As I sit here wondering about a place called Saginaw Bay. A place called Flounder Hill. A place called We Also Cherish Words That Remind Us of Our Ancient Ones. A place called But This Is the Way It's Always Been Done.

⊹ ‖ ⊹

Sleeping on Mabel's couch was as bad as or worse than sleeping in the church basement. The only scrutiny he'd had to endure in his cardboard enclosure was when the pastor inspected the door and cabinet locks on his twice-daily rounds. For the few weeks he'd slept in that basement, he could at least feel like the shopping bags he stuck under his cot were safe and unpried. Here at Mabel's, everything he did or said or left in a bag was examined and weighed and poked and tucked away in her steel-trap mind for interrogation over hardboiled green balls of brussels sprouts during the next strained uncomfortable dinner. But Patricia was happy to see him in the morning and happy to have him there to say goodnight to her at bedtime and happy to pop up out of nowhere for a quick hug and a stolen peck on his whiskered cheek before Mabel had a chance to tell her to finish her homework or take her bath or put away the clean dishes or sweep and mop the kitchen floor or wash her dirty hands and this time get them clean.

Nowadays he came home after work just in time for dinner. He washed his hands in the bathroom sink, rinsed off his face, folded and smoothed the towel back on its rack exactly as it had been, making sure it was creased and positioned right in the middle of the rack—the shorter rack, not the longer one, which was reserved only for bath towels of the same color and design as the hand towels and washcloths—placing the towel back at precisely the same distance from one shiny brass knob as was from the other. Most of the time after he got it right he'd see that he'd left fingerprint marks on the polished rung, and he'd have to wipe the almost imperceptible blotches off with toilet paper, fold the tissue back into a V, colorful flower design face up, wipe his sweaty tingling palms on the side of his pants, fortify himself with a deep sigh, and enter the kitchen to brave the night's dinner. These days his hands always felt dirty.

"There you are, Thomas! We were just about to knock on the door! Is everything all right?"

"Yes, everything's fine." Thomas settled into the polished ladderback chair at one end of the table, looking directly across at Mabel, Patricia on his left, scooted as close as she could get to him without Mabel telling her to scoot herself back. "Thanks." He checked out the plates. "It looks good."

"Thank you, Thomas! Patricia and I made something special tonight, since it's the three-month anniversary of your being here with us and almost six months since you've been sober. It's somewhat of a celebration." She pushed a platter of cooked green peppers stuffed with ground meat and rice toward him. "Have some of my family recipe, Thomas. Stuffed green peppers topped with our own secret recipe for tomato sauce." She ladled red liquid from the gravy boat and handed it to Patricia, who sat staring at the plate of cooked green peppers. "Take a pepper, Patricia, and cover it with a spoonful of the tomato sauce you and I made together." She nudged the platter toward Patricia's whitened hand. "Or would you like me to do it for you, dear?"

Patricia looked at Mabel's hands, then Mabel's face, then Mabel's dish. She cut her green pepper in half, exposing the hamburger mix that Mabel had allowed her to stir. She poured sauce over the mix and handed the boat to her dad.

"Don't forget your napkin, Patricia. It goes on your lap if you recall." Mabel smiled at Tom. "She's turning into quite a young lady, isn't she, Thomas?"

"She's my little girl. Thank you, honey," he said to Patricia. "This sauce looks good. Did you make it?"

"No. I stirred it once and then I helped stir the hamburger. It smelled pretty good while we were cooking it." She poked the green pepper mix with her fork. "I don't know about now, though."

"Now, Patricia," Mabel said. "This is our special dinner for your father." She evaluated the girl with a measuring gaze. "Remember your napkin, dear. It goes on your lap."

Tom slipped his own napkin onto his lap while Mabel was still watching Patricia.

Mabel and Tom had taken to going for little walks after Patricia was settled in bed, following the same route every evening, keeping an eye on the weather and, week by week, watching the growing daylight change the transplanted flowers in the gardens of the houses along the way. They turned right and strolled up to the corner, glancing at the governor's mansion—once or twice Mabel swore that she saw the governor walking his dog on the street ahead of them. She was always full of stories about her job in the building where the legislature met, where she typed and filed and gossiped and wondered about the lives of the men who traveled to Juneau from points all over the state. Her talking went on especially long after the rare times when the governor had passed by the door of her office. On those days when the governor popped in to say hello or to invite them to an open house, she wouldn't talk about anything else for hours. Tom always tried to humor her excitement, but a man is just a man, and the governor had no more relation to his life than any other of those suit-and-tied strangers who spent their time making up laws that controlled everything Tom could own, everything he could do, everywhere he could go, everything he could ever hope to be. Those laws, he had found, took away his freedoms and his rights, and gave him fines and court dates and jail time in return.

"Look at those beautiful azaleas coming into bloom," Mabel said. "They remind me of the flowers that grew in our yard when I was a girl." She turned away and walked a little faster. "Sometimes I still miss my mother."

"I don't remember my mother," Tom said. "Maybe it's worse to remember something and then lose it." He touched her arm, hoping to offer her some comfort. At his touch, her walk slowed again. As they turned the first corner, her cool thin fingers slipped inside the palm of his relaxed hand, where she found warmth. They walked to the overlook and stood there looking down on the village, holding hands. Three days later she beckoned him into her bed.

Mabel had no one to apologize to and nothing to explain. She still kept a clean house, her appearance remained always tucked and always tidy, and every single one of her meals was precisely on time. She went to bed at a proper hour and attended church in her appropriate Sunday best, always clean and newly pressed. If anyone questioned her decision to invite a deserving sober man to enjoy the comforts of a well-run home so he could spend time with his only child they could bring those questions to her and she'd be glad to give them their what for. Nobody asked.

Mabel carried a concern about the landlord. When she'd set Patricia up in the spare room—Mabel was glad now that she'd gone ahead and taken the larger apartment available in that desirable neighborhood, a two-bedroom unit, even though at the time she'd been afraid it could perhaps be seen by some as a bit indulgent—Mabel moved her few extra things out of the spare bedroom, spread crisp sheets on the unfolded cot, topped it with her mother's quilt she'd packed and carried with her over the years and across the miles, and perched a colorful clown lamp on the scratched but still serviceable dresser. "There!" she smiled at the girl. "Tomorrow we'll get you a few more clothes and send you back to school!" She arranged the lamp to aim the clown's gaping smile at the soft clean pillow where Mabel had pictured Patricia resting her head in comfort and gratitude, her now-washed hair framing her dear little Native face.

The girl stood stiff in borrowed pajamas, silent and tired. Her belly was full and her body was scrubbed. She couldn't think past falling into the bed. Mabel disappeared into her own bedroom and the sounds of rustling pierced the girl's awareness as she stood at the bedside, unmoving. Mabel returned, a dark brown flannel bear held tightly in her grip.

"Here, child." She folded the corners of the bedclothes and arranged the worn bear on the ruffled pillow. "Sleep here, dear. This was my quilt when I was your age. This bear was my best friend for many years. In point of fact, dear, he was my only friend."

Patricia allowed Mabel to guide her to the bed and tuck her into the cool sheets. Mabel pulled the quilt up to cover the girl's neck and stood for a moment looking down on the dear lost girl.

"Do you want me to leave the light on for you, Patricia?" she asked.

"No, it's okay," Patricia answered. "You can turn it off."

"All right then, dear. I'm leaving the door open just a little in case you need to call me for anything." In the leftover light of the living room lamps, Mabel could see the poor dear girl holding the stuffed bear, her knees bent, her face behind the bear as though she was kissing the top of its head. Mabel tiptoed out, certain that the girl was already asleep after the meal and bath and clean clothes Mabel had so generously provided out of the goodness of her own heart. She sat in the living room for a few minutes, no more than half an hour, just to be sure that Patricia didn't suddenly wake with a nightmare of the tawdry life that were it not for Mabel she would still be suffering. At her regular time, she rose to prepare herself for bed. She made a mental note to notify the landlord that another tenant would be occupying her apartment. She resolved to adjust her schedule to accommodate the needs of her newly rescued dear girl, surely one of the great good works of her life.

A few minutes after the light from Mabel's bedroom clicked off, Patricia crept to her door and hushed it shut. She waited a moment and slipped back to her bed feeling a little safer behind the now-closed door. She fell asleep hugging the worn stuffed bear, dreaming of her mother, longing for her dad. For the rest of her long, bumpy life, she harbored an unhappy fear of clowns.

Tom didn't know what to think when, glancing at a sound from the opening door, he saw Mabel standing in the sliver of dimmed light. He sat up. When she slyly put one finger to her furrowed lips in a gesture of be quiet, he froze. With that same finger, she beckoned him toward her.

Hesitantly he stood. They stared at one another across the expanse of her world. After some moments' deliberation, he stepped in her direction. It felt like when a man was deer hunting and caught sight of a doe or a buck, the distance between the man and the deer growing narrow not by design nor by action but by fate. It felt like when a woman was berrypicking and from behind the next patch of blueberries out popped a brown bear, the two staring at one another without a blink, locked in a gaze made not of design nor of action but of fate. It felt like when a white woman was calling a Native man into her bedroom, and the death grip she'd had on his generations and his stomach would now reach into his groin and from there into his heart not by fate but by her own actions and by her own design.

She was more than he could have wondered. She offered him comfort and rest. The smell of her sweat and the disorderly murmurs she tried so hard to repress made him feel like a man at last. Her body was generous by its own resolve, belying her meticulous budgets and grocery calculations. He would never tire of running his hands along her smooth ample curves. He would never tire of burying his face in the crook of her neck. He would never tire of bedtime with this woman now his woman Mabel.

He was finished with his dreams of the wild drunk girls down at the bar. He was finished with his longing for Lucille to come back and love him again like she used to say she did. He was finished with feeling apologetic for not being a good father on Mabel's terms. In her body-warmed bed, he was a man.

✴ ‖ ✴

Old Tom ambles along the beach. He feels thirsty. Nowadays he doesn't get thirsty the way he used to when he was drinking—that old sick thirst stronger than the retching need for nourishment—he gets thirsty these days for water. Usually cold fresh water trickles from the remnant of a once-abundant waterfall that continues to find its way to the beach near the button of a cove that Old Tom has come to consider his home. But at the close of a dry summer, only a bit of water wets the rocks one drop at a time. Old Tom would have to lick the rocks to get satisfaction. Such an endeavor will no longer satisfy his compelling thirst.

Old Tom remembers a bossy old neighbor near the house where he once lived, in those days when he lived in a house.

In those days when he had a family, children, warmth, food. Fresh water. That know-it-all neighbor always kept a flask in a trunk next to an old brown couch in the front room. That neighbor always slept on that brown old couch. He always kept one hand on the trunk inside of which was always that bottle.

Old Tom used to visit that old neighbor now and then hoping for a nip. He used to think hard about that bottle in those days when wine and beer and humiliation drove his concentration. He used to think hard about that bottle. Not so much about his own house that was once next-door to this neighbor, his old house that once held family, children, food. Warmth. A house that held its own fresh water.

Old Tom leaves his button of a cove and strolls over to Village Street, still thirsty. On the packed-dirt road he notices dried-up flat cakes of dogshit. Some things never change. With a shred of newspaper he keeps constantly in his pack, Old Tom scrapes the dogshit off his shoes. He knocks on the old neighbor's door.

Old Tom's neighbor opens the door, suspicious but as lonely as any of them. Old Tom invites himself in. They sit around for a while. It turns out the old neighbor has tried to sober up many times but can't get away from that bottle he keeps in his trunk. He sips from a bright purple cup, the winey stink of which now turns Old Tom's stomach and makes him more thirsty than ever for the taste of fresh water.

When that neighbor falls asleep, Old Tom notices that he is still holding that shred of newspaper in his hand, that package of dogshit. He thinks of how in the old days he would have smeared it on his neighbor's pants for a joke. He laughs. He waits. He keeps his eye on that once-beloved trunk.

That old neighbor finally wakes up. He wrinkles his nose. He probably smells the dogshit. Old Tom asks for permission to enter the back of the house. Of course, the neighbor agrees. Of course. Old Tom tucks the dogshit into the can in the bathroom that has been kept there all this time for just that purpose. He rinses his hands with cold medicinal tea from a cup on the rim of the sink. He scrubs his hands with leaves from the bottom of the chipped but still useful cup. Now his hands no longer smell like that dried up old dogshit.

Old Tom accepts the neighbor's offer of fresh cold water from the kitchen. He takes a drink. He tastes the fresh water. It might not be as fresh as the water that comes from a little waterfall in a button of a cove, but it is fresh and it is cold. He satisfies his thirst for a while, thanks his neighbor, and takes his cordial leave.

Old Tom walks into the woods up the hill from the village. He climbs over a path through the trees. Beyond the treeline and past the snowline he spits out water into the air. From above the clouds and the sky, from above the village and its people, he spits out fresh water to the world.

※ ‖ ※

The end of another fall. The beginning of another winter. Still living in that old trailer that had once been a sign of progress, of hope, of turning in a new direction. It felt cold enough for the first real fire of the season, one meant to warm the suddenly cool air, this already old house, these inevitably aging bones.

Since I'd come back home over twenty years before, I'd hoped to move back downtown to the Juneau Indian Village, back to the place where I was raised. But like Tlingit society itself, the Juneau Indian Village and its residents had been re-named, removed, relocated, and redefined. Summer villages once were places where people lived for a while, gathering the summer's wealth for later use then relocating to a milder winter village. For a while after American intervention, Tlin-git families continued to make traditional use of locations near and far, growing gardens in sunny areas, constructing smokehouses and campsites, maintaining fishing, hunting, and berry-picking sites. But it wasn't long before more and more laws intended to restrict and eventually abolish Native rights were forced on Tlingit people, appropriating their an-cestral land and restricting their ancestral freedoms.

Clan rights to summer and winter sites were seized by the territorial government to be given to non-Native settlers, mining companies, dairy farmers, any white person who could travel to the territory. My great-grandfather and his wife lost the family garden at Auke Bay and the smokehouse on Douglas Island.

One of the many laws created to appropriate personal and clan property was the Townsite Act, under which the Juneau Indian Village was formed by the territorial court. One tiny parcel, owned by the federal government in restricted status on behalf of my great-grandfather, delineated what was left of our family's land rights. Under the terms of the Townsite Act, each succeeding generation, no matter the number of children and grandchildren, shares ownership of the original property, which most often results in smaller and smaller fractions of the piece of land.

Over the years that my mother and I were living outside Alaska, the house where my great-grandmother had lived, where my grandmother had lived, where my mother had lived, where I had lived, was neglected by my uncle, the only family member still in Juneau, and demolished by the tribe. By the time my generation inherited title, ownership was shared by five descendants in varying fractions. Nothing can be built on the property, no use can be made of it, without express written permission by every named person. All transactions must be done according to federal laws. In my case the tribal practice was to grant this kind of assistance only when the help I was asking for was fully funded and specifically described in the paperwork, and then only reluctantly and after years of phone calls and messages.

After I'd been teaching for several years, after I gave up on ever finding my way through the deliberate maze of bureaucratic tribal and federal rules and regulations created by my inherited one-third interest in the fractionated Indian townsite that had been meant to house a family home, after I'd finally made the last payment on the third-hand mobile home I'd bought several years before, I found a triplex for sale on Gold Creek, no more than a block from where our old house had once stood. I cut my way through the many mortgage and property assessment tangles and made a solid offer. The property needed a lot of work and had been for sale for more than a year, so I felt confident that I'd found a family home. But the volunteer fire department that held the title withdrew it from the market, presumably to take care of the many needed repairs that the assessor's report had revealed, and I allowed those dreams to disappear like trails of unwelcome smoke drifting from an undamped fire. Other disappointments visited me that year, most significantly the children I helped raise. Ordinary rebellion, commonplace trauma, mundane heartbreak continued to mark my generations.

It rained again that day. A strong wind had blown the night before, and now winter announced itself in clean crisp air and reddened fingers. I'd built a fire in the woodstove and coaxed it with kindling and logs that my sons, now making their homes in Juneau, had piled in the arctic entry. It hadn't taken long for the fire to start crackling.

Flames have always given me energy and peace of mind and hope. Most likely, that comfort traces back to my childhood in our house in the old village, where my grandmother made toast for me on the woodstove in the kitchen, where she warmed my clothes on cold mornings before I left for school, where a kettle of deer meat stew simmered on fortunate days. Tending my fire these many years later, I was filled with acceptance that this wouldn't be the year I moved back to the village, and this would likely not be the year when the ones who come after me found a different path. But on that day I was filled, once again, with the hope that comes with outside rains and inner fires.

FOUR

They Are Holding Everything for Us

INSIDE THAT OLD MAN'S HOUSE, darker now by the measure of the starlight that has so recently brought ease to the outside world, the remaining two boxes of light begin to vibrate and pulse. The glow of their lately reawakened alarm hums renewed life into the walls, casts a growing light into the shining corners and upon the beaded blankets and over the woven baskets in which have been stored tomorrow's dryfish, next week's seal grease, next month's dried black seaweed, next year's reasons to live.

So many people have now come and gone there is hardly room to warm themselves by the memories of their fire. There is barely room for everyone to crowd around the flame, waiting for the food and warmth that will be sent by those they have left behind. When food is cast into the fires set by the loved ones they have left, the people in the house can eat. When the flames of the fires set by the loved ones they have left rise up to reach toward their already sunlighted world, the people waiting in the old man's house are warmed, their passions heated, their strength renewed. Now they can wait a little longer for that time when they will once again be released with the coveted daylight.

At the back of the old man's house, a spider finds her careful way to the edge of the wakening screen.

One scrap of earth, covered in snow. One cabin upon it, covered in snow. Inside, a woman solicits the fire's embrace. Even her minor needs are fading; one veined hand lifts one dried split log and makes it comfortable on top of the moss and kindling and twigs already beginning to burn. Soon the cast iron will warm itself and then the room and finally the woman's old bones. Soon the remnant of a shortened day will bathe her in dimmed blinding light. Soon it will be time to walk into the snow-covered forest. Outside, the raven cries.

Under her cover of snow, the earth seems to be asleep, but she remains vigilant. She simply yields. She simply waits. Her patience might be misleading, but she lingers in effortless calm. She is content only to be ready.

Do you see the glacier beyond the falling snow, resting in the arms of the distant mountains? It has overcome its patience and thinks now only of its own state of being ready. Ready to respond, ready to act, ready to wait. Ready to be aware.

Be like that glacier. Be ready like that glacier. Do not think of what you might do. Do not think of what you might not do. By thinking of nothing, you contemplate everything. When forces oppose, victory will be kind to the one who crafts herself like that glacier, to the one whose rest has been seasoned into vigilant repose.

Take Raven. He may have seemed at many times caught off guard, but he was always ready for whatever the moment would bring. When Raven held the daylight inside his attentive beak, he had probably not planned that his own loving grandfather would think about commanding his smoke-spirits to catch and hold Raven in the smokehole, as they both knew had already been done by another in an attempt to protect fresh water. When Raven held the daylight inside his attentive beak, it must then almost have seemed to him that a loving grandparent could also think about being stern. No matter. Raven's expectation that he would fly out that smokehole could not have caught him unprepared, even in the moment of his greatest trust. By this and others of his many examples, Raven teaches us that to be unplanned is not to be unprepared.

Though he must have feared that once again the smoke-hole spirits were about to envelop him, though the smoke-hole itself must have seemed to conspire against him, though the smoke from his grandfather's fire—the fire that had warmed his grandfather's daughter while Raven slept in her belly, the fire that had cooked the food that nourished his grandfather's daughter while Raven called for more and more to satisfy his unfilled hunger, the fire that had kept the darkest shadows of the darkest nights away from his bed in moments when even a treasured plaything was not enough to offer comfort, when only the promise of another day, only the hope of another tomorrow, could console—though even the smoke from that fire must now have stung his eyes and sooted his feathers and threatened to disquiet his escape, nevertheless Raven faced and dealt with his unexpected circumstance with daring and aplomb. These are the things that Raven did to break free and achieve his goal: he resisted, he battled, he prevailed.

✦ ❙ ✦

I rise before dawn, as is normal in short northwinter days. The light of the liberated moon coldly bathes the frozen trail. Bright lamps are lighted to warn the day that I am prepared. After some time, gray daylight turns itself into blue morning, and I turn down the lamplight in favor of the newly released day.

In summer months the night does not achieve deep darkness and the lights inside my home are seldom lit—only a small lamp here and there in the evening to ground me to the house. Without it, I might float away into the heavy summer sunlight. Into the midnight sun. But this is winter, and the day is crisp and bright. I leave burning only two dim lamps, one at each of the places I am likely to sit and chance to read.

The day wears on. A few more lamps are added and then the kitchen is made as bright as can be, for washing and chopping and cooking. But when the winter stew is left to simmer, the lights are dimmed again. Only one bright light over the stove continues to glow. This cycle of light inside the house reflects its own design. It is as predictable as any brilliant vision, as unsurprising as any miraculous dark.

Another winter day and it's morning again. Today's walk will take me away from the shore. The day is bright. Yesterday's snow glitters; the polished sky has subdued the wind for a while. This morning's chores and last season's errands have all been fulfilled and now is the time to take the path that will lead me into the forest. As I walk, my eyes are drawn toward the mountains.

The snow-covered trees that blanket the steep mountain, stretching themselves toward the clear bright sky, allow themselves to appear silent. I pause on my way to the edge of the forest. Once I am walking among the trees, I will not be able to see anything but the forested ground, the bare patches of earth beneath the hemlock, the forest itself. Before I take those steps, I must soothe my eyes one last vivid time with the sight of a sparkling mountain. I am filled with the vision of comforting cold, and as I wait in helpless wonder, a puff of white-dusted gray surrounds one tree in the midst of all the trees standing in their own helpless wonder on the mountain's slope. The tree below it is at once surrounded by another puff of dusted snow. The tree above it joins its silent powder to the quiet chorus. As do the trees below. Soon all the trees up and down the face of the mountain are covered in blurred softened gray. As I watch, the snow-covered trees transform the mountain itself into a cloud. I turn away from my walk. Although I know I will soon be called into the forest, today is not that time.

✤ ‖ ✤

More than wolves and bear now sleep beneath our layered scrap of earth. More than mosses. More than last summer's fallen leaves. More than last fall's berries, now dried and shrunken but bearing within them the comfort and promise of tomorrow's generations. More than last year's ashes, remnants of last year's long-dreaded deaths that no matter how late their arrival could only surprise. More than all of last year's memories. All of the things that have gone before us now lie beneath our treasured scrap of earth, but even though they seem to sleep, still they are at the ready. They are ready to enter that old man's house, ready to explore the darkness, ready to grab a carved and treasured box and fly through that smokehole no matter the struggle and bring back their light to the world.

After the end of fall, after the autumn harvest, after we've gathered and waited and practiced the fire and the ever-later dawn, all we can do is remind ourselves to be ready. Even the spruce and hemlock have bent themselves to the inevitable cold. Eagles that can bear to leave this place have left. Ravens have bunkered down. Mosses have either gathered themselves against the frozen soil or have allowed themselves to be collected for the cabin's fire. In any case, everything remains ready. Only the woman wonders if she can endure this season with the proper regard. The spruce and hemlock, the mosses, the eagle and the raven, do not make tomorrow's plans but only wait. Only the woman wonders if she will be here to welcome the spring that will surely follow in its season.

Now that the wood has long been gathered and carved into tables and boxes in which to store tomorrow's wealth, it's time to stoke the smoldering logs into a bed of cadenced coals. High flames might make us proud, but heat comes from a fire's embers. We build our strength in the way we build these coals, hoping that the flashes of youth and lust and passion will transform themselves into the glowing long-lasting heat that can carry us into one more spring and our children and our grandchildren into another summer.

Our utmost patience, our strongest yielding, our best plans come to nothing when we are not ready to avail ourselves of unexpected circumstances. No one can say when a given thing will occur, no one can say what path the coming flood will follow, nor how long its duration, nor how great its final depth. No one can say that there is always only one choice, that once we have resolved to be steadfast in our yielding, we must never consider another opportunity, we must never avail ourselves of changing circumstances should they arise to meet our last desperate hope. Instead, we must conserve our strength against the moment when all that seemed lost can now perhaps be salvaged with one flutter of the moth's wing waiting for the light, with the tremble of only one feather, only one glance from a spider making its way across the face of one smooth screen.

Take Raven. Although he'd been resting and eating and amusing himself with playthings from carved boxes, we can trust that his strength was never exhausted, his attention never so concentrated that he was not prepared to recognize opportunity should opportunity arise. Surely he knew that as soon as the shadows in his grandfather's house began to fade in the light of emancipated moon and unbound stars, it would be time to make his boldest move. Surely at that eternal moment when that old man caught a glimpse of Raven's uncovered truth, at that moment when Raven recognized that he was undone, he must immediately have chosen another strategy to take him away with little loss to himself and no loss to the world, loss only to his unhappy mother and to the loving grandfather who, seeing his dearest grandchild making off with his most cherished bentwood box of treasure, must have been willing to forfeit every luminous filament of his long-defended wealth for only one more moment of his grandbaby's honest smile, only one more moment of his grandchild's grateful embrace, only one more precious moment of his grandson's whimsical promises. But this life would never again present those brilliant moments for that old man's ready solace. It was no longer he who controlled his grandson's path. If, that is, he ever did control the path of Raven's actions, the path of Raven's choices, the path of Raven's thoughts. No matter. Despite all his grandfather's sorrow, despite his grandfather's disappointment, it was only Raven who now defined the direction in which Raven himself would proceed. Like all of us, it was only Raven who had ever defined his own path.

Inside that old man's house, now seemingly darker still, this time darkened by the measure of the absent moonlight that has now brought comfort and promise to the outside world, the remaining box of light can hardly be contained. Many of the people warmed by those fires lit by the loved ones they left behind and filled by food sent to them by loved ones so carefully tending their memories have at last returned to their clans along with the hoped-for daylight.

At the back of the old man's house, a spider makes her careful way toward the edge of the now-brilliant screen.

⁕ ‖ ⁕

Old Tom saunters along the beach. He hears curious sounds that seem to be emanating from a shell. He investigates. A clam shell, fully closed, of admirable size, is resting right here on the beach.

Old Tom picks up the clam shell. Holds it to his ear. His ear used to be winey all the time, but since he's been sober, he hasn't been hearing too many things that can be said to have come from drinking Tokay. Nevertheless, a moment ago he heard sounds that made him curious, and now he has found a clam right here on the beach not far from his button cove.

Old Tom often wishes he had brought Young Tom to this place. Even though Old Tom realizes that he was almost never able to find this particular place when he was drunk or when he was hungover, and Old Tom and Young Tom were not often sober at the same time, still it is a tender regret that Old Tom brings out to warm over the fire on exceptionally lonely days. It's too late now. It's probably even too late to bring Patricia here, but who can tell. Perhaps Old Tom will start hoping that one day he might bring all his generations to this button of a cove.

Old Tom shakes the shell. He considers prying it open. He remembers the taste of raw clam: salty, rich, juicy, cold— cold from the sea on a bright warm day, breeze and distant mountains, gulls and sea lions and egg-fat fish.

And clams. Old Tom pries open the clam. He is not surprised to find salty rich juicy clam meat. He is not surprised at the sudden mouth-filling succulence he thought he had forgotten. He is not surprised at the joyful acquiescence of the clam as he washes it down his gullet with its own juice. Old Tom is not surprised at the strength that courses immediately through his veins, that makes his arms feel sturdy and his groin come awake, that makes the light rain more welcome than ever and the forest join him in singing his thanks. The taste of this clam has made Old Tom come alive, and Old Tom is not surprised.

Patricia's mother, Lucille, blew back into town one early morning and showed up at her favorite bar as though she'd only been gone for a few quick days. Old Tom sat inside enjoying a cup of free coffee sweetened by the bartender's conversation and a clear sober head. In walked Lucille.

She took a stool at the end of the bar, where her view of passersby was unobstructed. To Old Tom, she looked the same as she had when she and his son were newly married, the same as she had when she ran around on the summer streets when his son was out fishing for a living for them both, the same as she had when she left their little girl Patricia home alone while she hunted for a party or for a man or for both, the same as he'd imagined her while he ached at his son's funeral, where he watched his granddaughter being comforted by Mabel's unbending solace, where everybody wondered why Lucille couldn't have shown up at a funeral service for the father of her child.

"Hey! Is that you, old man?" Lucille motioned the bartender for another glass. "Have some beer from my pitcher, you mooch!" She poured foamy beer into the second glass, checked the sidewalk, smiled into the dull mirror, and with one gulp emptied her own glass of morning vigor.

Old Tom carried his cup out of the shadows at the end of the bar. He stood two stools away from Lucille and motioned away her outstretched hand. "No, thanks," he said. "I'm sober now."

"Sober! I never thought I'd see that day!" She emptied the second glass, wiped her lips with the back of a hand, poured another drink from the half-empty pitcher. "My beer's half-gone already, old man. Sure you don't want just one little drink?"

"You still have plenty left. If I change my mind I'll let you know." He leaned his elbow against the curve of the bar. Most of the town's morning workers had already rushed by the window. It was too early in the day for tourists to give any sort of show. The street-washers had rinsed last night's butts and blood into the gutter and had disappeared along with their sweepings. For now, there was nothing to look at but each other. Old Tom waited.

Lucille rationed herself another serving of beer. She raised the sweating glass to her lips and held it there for a minute. Then another minute. Then another. Old Tom waited.

Lucille finally took a sip and put down the glass. Old Tom watched the bartender busying himself in the shadows at the other end of the long counter, shining the surface, polishing the tap, arranging the colorfully labeled bottles against the mirror. It was slow so far this morning, but everybody knew that sooner or later it would change. Old Tom thought about the picture they presented: one sobered-up old drunk and a random middle-aged woman with a few dollars and chipped red fingernails, dressed in a low cut blouse that divulged her sagging breasts. One man, one woman, both determined. She on her way to getting drunk, he on his way to staying sober. The morning might be slow, Old Tom knew, but business was bound to pick up.

⁘ ‖ ⁘

It's the time of the year when eagles die. Friends tell of carcasses by the stream; eagles pick at rice thrown out for hungry ravens. Snow is melting, but no fish are here to soften the eagle's hunger. The helpless young of tasty prey are still nuzzled in their mother's careful embrace. The eagles will eat whatever they must to survive, but their distaste at the cold bloodless grain is clear. Eagles are meant to kill.

Han Shan's Red Cliffs, Harjo's Oklahoma, Momaday's Rainy Mountain, Hiroshige's Edo. If I were to take up Hiroshige's project and portray *One Hundred Famous Views of Lingit Aani*, with what image would I begin? The perfect silhouette of which mountain would form the background to the scene of seeking, chasing, and searching for the coming season's first salmon? Along the banks of which river would the people be lined, ready with their drums and their voices to welcome their relative home from his long journey, trusting that he would send word of this warm welcome back to his brothers and his sisters?

My scenes would not attend to the celebrating crowd but rather the lone observer who stands in the shadow of the celebration, who lives at the edge of the crowd, who poses at the brink of the procession. That procession would not be somber, those songs would not be mournful, that laughter would be loud. Yes, such games are meant for children. Love is meant for the young. War and loneliness are designed for all.

My little cabin on a small patch of earth rests its soul in sunlight, washes its face in rain, wraps its arms around itself in the cold. My cabin on its patch of wet earth settles itself to await the unavoidable dawn.

Silent fishing boats listen for herring fat with roe. What is there but water? With what shall a mountain be covered if not by snow?

Meanwhile, a tree not yet in blossom flirts in vain with the windblown ribbons, and a lone woman living in a cabin on one tended scrap of earth makes herself ready to greet the inevitable spring.

Although I am filled with admiration for each newly gray hair at my brow and each dry fine wrinkle at the back of these worn hands that have comforted children and caressed lovers and wiped my own tears from my face in the worst times of brittle loneliness, I know that in this life I will never again be as young as I am today. Each eternal moment, each passing day, each transient year, each priceless smile from one who has never been and will never be anything but my tender child constitute the greatest examples of my wealth, and I now recognize that with the accumulation of age most of my treasure has been spent.

Yet not spending treasure is only one of the four elements of victory. Conserving comfort and love and consolation is accomplished by letting them go. Riches are doubled by their distribution. Food and goodwill are sent to the next world when opposites are made full with the provision of our best late-summer nagoonberries, our most deliciously smoked red sockeye, our warmest fine-woven blankets. Everyone who seeks wisdom will sooner or later come upon this truth.

❉ ‖ ❉

The people who came before us were practiced in devious warfare. Take the story of the one-hundred-year war, which began when a woman left her husband for a man from another village. The first husband could not simply turn away, even though one can suppose that he was glad to be rid of a woman who practiced deviousness not in matters of war but in matters of love. It was his purpose now to restore balance. It was now incumbent upon him to reclaim his honor as openly as that woman and that man had openly caused him shame.

After the first disastrous attempt to regain honor, the next generation was raised to blame all unwelcome circumstance on the people of that other village. When the time finally came to invite them to make peace, retribution was accomplished and honor was restored. With this example and others like it, we can take some comfort from the knowledge that even though it may take some generations, we can and we will turn away from the brink. We will be cunning with our treasure and practical in our choices. We will persevere; we will overcome; we will be open and unknowable.

⬩ ‖ ⬩

My grandmother was always a tough old woman ready for any challenge. Even after my mother and I left Alaska, even after we heard news of her death, even after I sat for hours with her memory, re-creating the years she had fed me soup and told me stories and washed my clothes, she was only the imposing, gray-haired woman who taught me I was Eagle, who told me bears were my cousins, who reminded me that the wind was my grandfather. She often declared that our family carried powerful names, but I never saw in her the youthful bearing that comes with the noble birth she claimed.

Recently, a Raven relative gave me a photograph I'd never seen. My grandmother poses with confidence, dressed in the latest white-man ruffles, her shoes, hair, and jewelry slick, modern, rich. Behind her, an embroidered cloth brushes against the polished arm of the leather chair upon which she rests her hand. Behind her could have been a flowered dish awaiting her dignified touch. She always favored decorated platters.

Before her was a path lined with years of tumult and sorrow. But in that moment, she must have thought that her station in the world she and her people were now forced to enter would be equal to the one she was leaving. She must have thought she could meet every new challenge. She must have thought she was entering a world where highborn Tlingit women were respected, where white-man ruffles danced like Chilkat fringe, where sunflowers could bloom in our dark rainforest gardens.

I haven't been taking good care of my loved ones. Feeding my opposites has become no more than a duty without the joy that duty brings when accomplished with compassion. My loved ones are seated around a cold fire wondering, Where is my fish? Where is my grease? Where is my descendant? My loved ones have been lingering in the cold ground, but spring is upon us and I will take up my responsibility, I will seek counsel on how best to bring back their names, I will joyfully give to my opposites the food I have prepared only for them. My loved ones will rejoice.

⁜ ‖ ⁜

Old Tom walks along the beach. The tide is high. He thinks about all the cunning traps that have caught almost everyone in their grip. How to tell a trap from the normal course of things? How to know when the answer is to escape or just to go along? Old Tom can consider only what he knows. He must leave the act of finding answers to those who are less curious than he.

Not long ago as time goes, Old Tom remembers, he heard of a virtuous man who forced himself into a woman's home and beat her nearly to death. Good thing he's such a good doctor, all of the neighbors said. But other persons, even some of those who loudly sang their good intentions, even some of those who had wrapped their gracious cloths around her bloody lacerations, resented the bandages and aspirin that the man took from their medicine cabinets to so charitably treat her life-threatening wounds. They turned away from her suffering to debate responsibility.

Some of her neighbors resented the dollars the man promised to spend to treat her father's alcoholism, her uncle's diabetes, her mother's cancer, her cousin's suicide, her sister's depression, her brother's abuse, all of her family's trauma. Neighbors drew the hems of their skirts away from her untidy suffering and chose to debate the nature of generosity from within their own sanitary homes and from inside their own whitewashed classrooms.

At the time, Old Tom wondered about those things.

Now, walking along the beach, Old Tom continues to muse. He decides that the beaten woman probably will not live or die according to the generosity of the man who beats her or according to the charity of those neighbors. Old Tom knows that the woman can endure in spite of those who harm her with worthy intentions and in spite of those who mean her deliberate ill. Bandages and aspirin will not save that beaten woman, Old Tom decides, but receiving those offerings with complacency can kill her. She can allow them to patch her together with sympathy and donations, but Old Tom knows that whether alone or with the help of her wounded family, she must fight hard for her own life.

Not long ago as time goes, a man forced himself into a woman's home and beat her nearly to death. If that woman or her relatives had thought to ask him, Old Tom would have counseled that she go ahead and accept bandages and aspirin but that she try hard to remember who she is. After she reclaims her own identity, Old Tom would have told them, she will be able to heal herself.

At the unexpected sound of a dry knock, Mabel peeked out the spy-hole and was aghast to recognize Tom's dirty ex-wife, Lucille, on the other side of the door. She wondered what on earth that woman wanted now. Probably money, she guessed. Just like Tom Senior used to do, both before and after Thomas died and his memory was put in the ground. Now that Tom Senior seemed to be staying sober, Mabel allowed him to see Patricia's children at regular intervals under her supervision for limited amounts of time, but she wouldn't let herself forget that alcohol abuse ran in that family from father to son to daughter and while it was part of her godly duty to minister to their needs and the needs of their poor dear helpless uneducated children, she was not going to encourage that sort of behavior by giving them handouts when they were drunk. She opened the door.

"Yes? May I help you?"

Lucille stepped back, straightened her shoulders. Mabel was glad to see her take a quivering half sigh.

"Are you Mabel?" Lucille wiped her mouth, her newly painted red nails flashing against brown skin. She cleared her throat and managed a horizontal smile.

Mabel stood taller. She brushed imaginary crumbs from her ruffled apron and held the door open by only a few inches. "Who are you?" she asked. She slid the toe of her spotless pump against the bottom of the door for extra protection. "Why did you knock on my door? Is there some way I can help you?" She glanced behind Lucille and down the hall. No surprise if this woman had brought some of her drinking cronies, just as Thomas so often had, just as Tom Senior had. Just as Mabel imagined Patricia would do if it ever occurred to Patricia to try to see the children.

"I was wondering if I could see my grandchildren," Lucille said. "I'm Patricia's mother. I was wondering if I could see them. If it's okay with you." She licked her lips. "If you would let me see them," she repeated.

They waited in silence, Lucille filled with powerless, half-formed expectations, Mabel holding all the cards. They examined each other from across the chasm, one with the poor hope that she might be allowed a glimpse of her grandchildren, the other with an entitled grip on the doorknob, the toe of one polished shoe holding the barrier shut.

"They're not here," Mabel told her.

Lucille waited. "Will they be back later?" she finally asked.

"Yes, of course they'll be back," Mabel replied. "They live here."

Lucille waited. "Can I come back later and see them?" she finally asked.

"I'll have to check. I keep them busy." Mabel told herself, not for the first time, that she should keep a pencil and notepad near the door just as she kept one next to the telephone. She resolved to add that item to her weekly list of things to do. Place a pencil and notepad next to the door, she imagined herself writing on the magnetized notepad she kept in the kitchen on the refrigerator next to the magnetized grocery list. She resolved to add sanitary hand wipes to the list, mentally placing them next to the notepad she would place next to the door. She should probably visit the mercy seat this coming Sunday on Lucille's behalf, and she supposed she should now also admonish the two dear children in her care to pray for the salvation of their grandmother as they did for their mother and their various siblings as the news and the needs arose.

Lucille waited. "Do you think I can come back and see them later today?" she finally asked again.

"No, not today," Mabel assured her. "Give me your telephone number and I will be happy to call and let you know if there's a good time for you to visit them."

"Even for a few minutes when they come home," Lucille said. "Even just to look at them, see how they look. Just see what they look like now." She fought the sting of tears. She didn't want to let this woman see her tears. "Even just to see how they look," she repeated.

"I'll let you know," Mabel said. "As I said, I keep them busy. It's for their own good. I'll check their schedule and I'll let you know." She shut the door.

⸭ ‖ ⸭

Although Raven could well have decided to keep light and luster and blinding brilliance for only his own pleasure, he knew that to keep riches to oneself guarantees their decline. In this regard, Raven was wiser than even that old man who had sought to hold those owned things in those hidden boxes and never show them to any but his own precious loved ones. That old man hadn't learned the human lesson that when we hold our precious owned things for only our chosen loved ones to be brought out and meted one by one as though to a crying child, the chances are great that our own loved ones will not respect the individual worth of our precious treasures and will steal them for themselves and for the world.

The urge to bring out light to show and give to his human opposites was too compelling for Raven to resist. There is nothing to make us suppose that Raven felt remorse or even compunction; indeed he appears only to have felt indignation at the thought that his own grandfather might seem to be willing to reciprocate Raven's betrayal. This is the way of the world. Such is the way of the generations.

How must Raven's grandfather have felt at the knowledge that his own grandchild had stolen from his store of treasure? Did that knowledge cost him far more heartbreak than losing his precious Box of Starlight, losing his cherished Box of Moonlight, losing his irreplaceable sun? And Raven's mother, what of her? How did that woman feel, after sheltering Raven in her womb for what would have been months if the moon had been free to calculate the passage of that time? At the instant that Raven burst through the smokehole with the final prize, at the instant of his escape, the light of the uncaptured sun, which he thought he carried but which was after all only using Raven to give itself to the world, must have ignited the air between the heartbroken old man and his suddenly old daughter and the glimpse they shared must have contained all the heartache of every mother and every father and every grandparent and every lover and every friend who has ever been betrayed.

Where is Raven's compassion? Preparation, resolve, patience—those attributes can be seen in Raven's behavior and deeds. Simplicity, adaptability—he exemplifies those qualities for those of us willing to contemplate the model of his complex virtue. But recognizing Raven's compassion is like stopping where another has walked through a shallow bit of water and waiting for the earth's clean dirt to settle and the water to become clear. Simplicity and patience are not difficult to recognize, but accepting the world without complaint requires trust.

Raven trusted the world, but he must also have trusted his own nature and his own purpose. He was moved by brilliant curiosity and by his illuminated desire to fling daylight into the sky. He was moved by his concern for people who, accustomed to the dark, did not even recognize their need for light.

A readiness to reflect on the sorrow of another's loss is not a virtue readily seen. We can only contemplate, consider, ponder, Raven's actions. We can only intuit the excellence of his purpose. But we do know that by some compassion he was moved to bring light to our dark world.

Inside that now dark house, an old man sits alone in the now-darkened shadows. He tries to overcome the sorrow that has been delivered by his beloved grandchild's deceit. He tries to clear his thoughts. He tries to accept the nature of this world. Take my treasure, he must think. I give it to you freely. I ask nothing from you except that you remain healthy and continue to live. I ask only that you do not kill me. And of these two things that I ask of you, for you to remain healthy is my greater wish. Remain healthy, and try not to kill me.

Outside that old man's now dark house, a woman sits alone in the lightening shadows at the edge of the once-dark stream. She longs for the sight of a pine needle floating toward her in the unclear waters, for the unfamiliar taste of the promise of a new tomorrow, for the sound of the voice of future generations crying for everything their outer shells can give.

⊹ ‖ ⊹

Lucille still went to the bar almost every morning, but only for coffee. This time she would stay sober. She stirred spoons of sugar and dabs of creamer into strong black coffee and thought about regrets and plans and hopes. She allowed herself to imagine visits with the grandchildren, making them laugh, discovering their favorite cereals and favorite dinners, bundling them to take them on walks to craft snow angels in the winter and to find a promise of salmonberries in July. She wanted the children to become her pastime, her sporting event, her life's welcome role.

She tried to imagine what Young Tom would have done had he lived. She wanted to remind the children that they had a grandfather who would have loved them, who would have taught them how to clean a fresh-caught fish in the summer, who would have brought fresh deer meat home in the winter, who would have held them above his head with strong arms and a joyful laugh, who would have wanted only the best for them no matter where they lived, whether it was with their own mom in some dreamed-of future, or with Mabel in the Fosbee Apartments on the hill above the Indian Village downtown.

In her long life—people like to say she's in her forties if she's a day—Lucille has made a lot of mistakes. Small, hard-kernelled mistakes hidden in the secret pockets of her memory, rolled now and then between metaphorical thumb and finger, tested against their unyielding shells. Slightly larger mistakes that she sucks on and chews and fiddles with like a still-sore tooth or dry socket. Really big mistakes to which the only honest reaction is denial. Like everyone, she's made a lot of mistakes.

And failures—grand failures, to be sure, failures so profound they can't be framed with words, failures that can be captured only in the briefest flash of a shattered image: a once-happy child, a too-hasty word, the profound reluctance to act, the accumulation of one bad choice after another, sorrows that too often ended up as no more than one more reason to drink.

Lucille's mistakes have been many and measurable. Pesky little rattails and unwanted mosquito toes, they show up unbidden and appear according to their own impulses. But her grandest failures—those have taken shape as vampires and chimeras. They have visited her in the forms of ghosts and nightmares and visions. They are lodged in her memories as the what-ifs of her life, as what she can't find the words to regret, the things she has invited to come close and to haunt her. She long ago accepted that she would leave mistakes behind in a littered trail of blunder. Her failures, though, she knows she will take to the grave.

Lucille's own mother had spent a lot of time in bars. She began to know about Lucille secondhand, began to hear about her antics and sicknesses and accomplishments and accidents from grudging family gossip. When Lucille's mother heard about all of those things, when Lucille's mother was too drunk, too busy having too much of a good time with too many friends to care to do anything about Lucille, Lucille supposed her mother must have taken another drink.

Lucille's memory of the last of her mother's confessions of failure happened in the weeks before her death. Lucille had been almost ten years old. "I know I've failed you," her mother told Lucille over and over, twisting in her dried-out deathbed, stroking and gripping Lucille's hand with chapped hands and reddened fingers. Their eyes met in the reflection of years of neglect. "No, Mom. That's not true. You loved me," Lucille protested. "I know you loved me, Mom." She held a glass of something sweet to her mother's dry lips.

And now, Lucille knows, she has failed her own daughter. She has disappointed her child's every hope. When Patricia had to get by on her own, it was because Lucille had let her down. Patricia's life has become a monument to all of Lucille's flaws, a mirror to all of her failures, a keepsake for all their shared regrets.

Patricia danced into the bar one morning fresh and early. She'd heard a few days ago that her mother was in town asking around about Patricia and the babies. She'd heard that Lucille was sober now and only patronized her favorite old bar for morning coffee. It might be well over ten years since Lucille had left her with the quick promise of peppermint, but Patricia still lived with the aching empty spot inside her, carved deeper every day by the memory of Lucille's silhouette in the doorway.

When things had changed between Mabel and her dad, they changed between Patricia and her dad, too. Mabel seemed to want to be the same good-works older friend she'd always tried to be, but Patricia could sense Mabel's glee when it was Mabel who got the first hug, the last kiss, the tender whisper into her delighted and expectant ear. Patricia geared up her claims, but that just made it easier for him to pull her grip away from his shirt, easier to tell her once and for all this was the last time tonight he was coming into her room to say goodnight, easier to chase her away when she tried to snuggle onto his lap, easier to leave without saying goodbye.

Nothing had been able to fill those hollow places, not all of Mabel's lessons in etiquette, not any of the beer or vodka Patricia had swallowed, not the triumph of love from one man and then another. Not even the flash of love in her children's eyes when she appeared for a visit in their doorway. Not even the sight of her long-gone mother, come back to her at last.

With a long-necked bottle of courage in her hand, Patricia approached Lucille, who was studying her slow-stirred coffee and hadn't yet looked up. "Mom?"

Lucille turned at the sound of her daughter's voice. She knocked over two stools when she jumped up. She grabbed Patricia in a hard embrace, hugging her and crushing her in a mother's loving arms. She held her daughter as tight as she could until the years began to soften.

At the end of two weeks, Lucille arrived at Mabel's door once again. In the minutes after she knocked, Lucille was convinced she heard someone creep to the other side of the door, would have sworn she saw a shadow cover the tiny peephole, was certain she recognized Mabel's unforgettable odor of perfume-covered sweat rising from under the door to assault Lucille's senses. When no one answered, Lucille pulled an already prepared note from her newly purchased bright-red faux leather purse, inside of which were treats and pictures for the grandchildren, and left the note for Mabel's sure attention. Kneeling to slip the lavender paper under the silent door, Lucille thought she could perceive not only the now stronger trace of perfumed sweat, but also the unmistakable scent of concern mixed with fear mixed with longing. Lucille pulled the paper back and with a purple sharp-point felt-tipped pen—also a new purchase—Lucille added to the message that gave her address and telephone number the invitation *Let's have coffee sometime* and cast her words upon the waters of Mabel's good intentions.

Mabel watched with horror as the torn page slid under her door, slid back out, and a moment later slid into her sight again. She waited at the door for another five minutes, timing herself by the watch she wore on her wrist, standing as still as she could and fighting an uncompromising urge to pee. She stealthily leaned her head toward the door and squinted through the fisheye lens. The hall was empty.

Mabel squatted on the floor to read the lavender note asking for permission to see the children and inviting her for coffee. Coffee indeed. Mabel was somewhat surprised that Lucille's new address was only a block or two away, on this very hill, in fact, quite close to the governor's mansion. Mabel was familiar with the string of houses along the hillside that looked down on the village, and she was certain that Lucille must have moved into the tiny efficiency apartment tucked into the lower level of the three-story house just before the corner, a house that looked down on the parking lot of the modern tribal building at the other end of the village.

Mabel had always wondered about that little apartment, had tried to imagine, had circumstances been different, had she moved there instead of to the Fosbee, whether she would have rescued Patricia, married Thomas, or adopted the children had she been comfortably ensconced in a cozy efficiency instead of the two-bedroom apartment that even now could sometimes feel hollow when the children were off on their activities and she found herself alone yet again. Perhaps Mabel would take Lucille up on her invitation after all, if only to take a closer look at that apartment. She placed the note next to the telephone, resolving to check her calendar and make a notation—in black ink, not some dreadful girlhood color—to call Lucille one day soon on behalf of the children's need to meet at least one of their other grandmothers.

At Mabel's sharp two-knuckled tap, Lucille hurried to the door. Even if her front door had sported one of those peephole gadgets, designed for spying, advertised for safety, used as a barrier, Lucille would have opened the door right away to greet her visitor. She pulled the door open to welcome Mabel with a smile and an invitation to coffee.

"Come in!" Lucille stepped back to wave Mabel into the apartment. "Have a seat! Do you want me to take your jacket?"

"No, I'm fine," Mabel replied. She assessed the little apartment.

A modest butcher-block dinette table snugged itself against a tidy casement window on the side of the building facing the hill. Lucille had set it with two cups, creamer, sugar, and an electric coffee pot. Mabel draped her jacket on a chair back and positioned herself to gaze out the window.

Lucille hurried into the kitchenette and opened the oven door. "The biscuits are done!" she exclaimed. "I'll bring them with some butter. I hope you like them."

Mabel could barely keep herself from gasping for air at the overwhelming aroma of fresh-cooked bread, the sudden sensation of the oven's friendly warmth, the sounds of someone else cooking in the kitchen. She took one deep breath and forced a smile. "I'm sure I will," she answered.

Lucille had found a butter dish and a set of two matching teacups at the thrift store only the day before. She placed paper napkins on the table and checked the sugar and creamer. She tucked the open curtains more securely in their sashes and took her seat across from Mabel. "Isn't this a nice view?"

"Yes, it's much better than mine. The wildflowers are lovely. And you can see the water from here." The bark of a distant dog made it feel even more like home.

"Do you want more sugar?" Lucille asked. "Can I get you some salmonberry jam? The other grandkids and I picked berries last summer and we froze them and put some up for jam and ate a gallon every day."

Mabel remained silent.

"It was a good year for berries," Lucille continued after a pause. "Maybe we can all pick berries together this year." She waited a moment. "If we all wanted to."

Mabel turned away from the view of the village below. "Yes," she said. "Yes, that would be nice. I'd like that."

✢ ‖ ✢

I began teaching an introductory class in creative writing and a pre-designed freshman seminar titled Sense of Place—since I was actually from the place, my appointment as an adjunct seemed logical to the professor in charge of temporary hires. The following year, I was awarded a one-year part-time appointment when a newly hired tenure-track professor unexpectedly resigned. Her upcoming course schedule, now mine, included Alaska Literature: Native and Non-Native Perspectives despite the fact that she had been in Alaska less than a year. She could hardly have gained insight into Native perspectives, and perhaps hadn't succeeded or even attempted any primary research on the subject, nevertheless everyone in power had agreed that a humanities PhD bestowed upon her the authority to teach Alaska Native perspectives in literature. I was bemused at their idea that Alaska Native perspectives could be so easily understood and taught, but I was not ungrateful for the chance of a job with a paycheck that could get me started on chipping away at the mountainous student loans and credit card balances I'd accumulated.

Non-Indigenous professors, artists, writers, scholars, storytellers, seamstresses, designers, speakers, and all those others who happen along and present themselves as authorities on anything to do with a colonized people—whether art, stories, or perspectives on literature—are engaging in appropriation and are normalizing colonial behavior. Retelling stories, producing artworks, and claiming Native identity are the most common methods by which non-Native people profit from the passive-aggressive routine of allowing others to believe that they are authorities on Indigenous subjects, or that they are themselves Native people. In spite of their protestations of respect, their citations of personal relationships, their exhaustive studies, all such practices are colonial acts.

Alaska has only recently been colonized, and its institutions reflect that recent misfortune. A significant percentage of incoming college students in Alaska are Alaska Native people, yet most faculty are not Indigenous; they are not people of color at all. But tenure-track faculty in all subjects, the majority of whom came to Alaska in response to an offered position, generally avoid first-year courses. Except, of course, Sense of Place.

The professor I was to replace didn't appropriate identity, but simply embodied colonial authority. The American educational system bestows that authority on those it was designed to exalt: teachers and professors who explain to trusting students the subjects they know mainly by theory and sometimes by observation, teachers and professors who have been trained in the Western model to perpetuate Western paradigms. They agree to do whatever they are asked to do, and in most cases they believe that their Western-designed credentials accord them the ability to do so. Still, I was more than willing to fill the unexpected vacancy, lucky to have it, happy to say yes. If the classrooms had been located on a vessel traveling the inland waters of Southeast Alaska, the offer would have been perfect.

I wonder about the sacrifices it must have taken for my mother to achieve any sort of success in her clerical career at the Bureau of Indian Affairs. In the years when she worked for Alaska statehood and then for the Bureau of Indian

Affairs, the specter of white bosses with their nonwhite help-
ers wasn't considered something to be remarked upon. For
the main part, it's still that way, but now that record is con-
demned with faint proclamations declaring the desire for
equity and with protestations that hiring committees just
can't find qualified people of color. Committees hold fast
to the artificial standards that were put in place to exclude
all others but themselves, and then those same committees
bemoan their ill luck. Too bad! they allow themselves to say,
and pretend to wonder at the problem, seeing nothing out
of the ordinary now that perpetuation of colonialism is the
norm.

My exhausted mother's universal moans, my grandmother's
Tlingit scolding—those might have been the first sounds that
crept into my hungry ears, but when it came time for me to
learn how to talk and what to say, I was taught to speak English, believed by Tlingit leaders to be the language of success.

My mother understood Tlingit but was not allowed to
speak it. My grandmother spoke to me in Tlingit and taught
me phrases and dances and songs, but she sent me to school
to learn the white man's words from white teachers. These
things cannot be denied; they simply happened. I still carry
those wounds. Some bruises don't heal.

Scholars who have earned a piece of paper declaring
them fit to dissect my story lay out my generations on a cold
table under harsh lights meant to keep me from rising. I am
covered by an antiseptic cloth and a curtain to prevent them
from seeing my face. White gloves protect their clean hands.
Their tender skin does not touch my opened belly, my beating heart, my rage.

I want to think I've done all I can, yet my own generations sharpen the scalpel. I choke down sweetened bile from the siren's gut. I mop up clever vomit. I ignore my own unbandaged wounds. I forge pennies to pin on my sunken eyes.

Slaughterhouse stink, asylum scream, the soothing melodies of oppression: We hum and dance to a death song decades long.

There's no doubt that it is important for Alaska Native students to see Alaska Native professors and administrators. In the struggle against colonialism, it's just as important for white students to see Alaska Natives and other people of color in positions of authority. In any institution situated in a colonized place, it is even more important for people in power to recognize Alaska Native intellectual authority.

Indigenous history, Indigenous philosophy, Indigenous intellectual understanding, are qualities that settlers and their descendants find threatening. Nevertheless, these are plain truths. I am here because of unacknowledged warriors like my mother and others like her, people who held their places in spite of injury and loss, in spite of cultural battery that would have undone others. Many families lost their art, their language, their history, their health, but they passed to us the awareness of power. We follow the footsteps of the walking wounded in this cultural war, and everything we are able to accomplish now we owe to them.

⊹ ‖ ⊹

"A world tour of Southeast Alaska," we called the project a fellow writer and I had been invited to undertake, visiting communities to read from and talk about our published works. We began on the Juneau campus, with an evening talk for the public, at which no one could deny that the favorite Anchorage nature writer—once from Southeast Alaska but now living in the dry American Southwest, where she joked it was a pleasure to say we need some rain and mean it—was the real draw. Anyone who wanted to see me could walk down the hall of the Soboleff Building, where I'd finally regained an office, or through the cafeteria, or past the art-filled library where my friend and I now sat on the platform, trading jokes and praising one another's work to a respectable crowd of mostly familiar faces. In two days it was off to Sitka and then to Ketchikan and finally by Inter-Island Ferry to the village of Craig on Prince of Wales Island before whirlwinding back to Juneau, where I'd pick up my classes where I'd left off.

In Sitka, where the tour wrangler had booked all three of us—herself, my fellow author, and me—into a single studio's living space for the night, my happiness about the tour hit a familiar snag. I had expected at least a private bed, since I had renounced my fee to contribute the in-kind portion of the grant. Our wrangler rushed across the street to secure me a room in the local hotel, and I told myself that adding to my growing reputation as a grump was a small price to pay to avoid a camping-out scenario, with beds only a few inches apart in a living space just off the open kitchen. My 5 a.m. coffee, I imagined, would not endear me to campmates who liked to stay up past midnight laughing over a few glasses of friendly red wine.

I sometimes wonder who I would have been had I lived one or two hundred years before this life. I see myself living in the rain forest, of course. Always in the rain forest. I can only imagine myself as a woman who lives in the blurred space at the edge of the village and the edge of the forest. A place where people might walk by on their way to other destinations, where I might hear their distant voices and smile at the sounds of their laughter and their gossip. Where one or two friends might occasionally stop by to share stories or tea or silent suspenseful wonder at a deer or eagle that has crept too close to the uncovered window.

My mother was somewhat of a recluse herself. In every way, I am becoming the woman that she was. A bit intimidating, I'm told, at least to the timid or to those who savor a colonial fear of the other. She was generous at times, she was stone-hearted at times, she was happy and private and full of vague regrets she tried not to think about, she tried not to recognize, she would never admit. A complex woman, as all women are complex.

To the end, my mother swore that my father was the only man she had ever loved. Other than that repeated declaration and an indistinct memory of being told I had his chin, the only information I received was the short bitter story that not long after I was born she unexpectedly saw him on the street—in my mind, that street is Willoughby Avenue, but her story didn't achieve that particular detail—and after asking him if he wanted to see the baby, received his bluntly negative reply. I understood that baby was me. I understood that man was my father. I understood he didn't love me. What I didn't understand until long past the hope of seeing her again in this life was that neither did that man love my mother.

After my mother was gone, I sometimes allowed myself

to wonder what might have happened had he peeked under that pink blanket, the one for which she had saved all her nickels and pennies, the baby blanket with the periwinkled hint, the blanket under which she had stored her hopes and newly learned prayers along with promises to be a godfearing Christian as-close-to-white-lady as she could get if he would only only only take a peek and fall in love with his precious baby daughter who smelled of hard-purchased talcum powder and the formula that was necessary because her pessimistic breasts had abandoned any hope of ever again bearing the pain of a rummaging nippled mouth full of self-interest and feigned love.

My mother must have realized she was pregnant about the time that Christmas was on its way. She was twenty-two years old. The traditional winter potlatches that her own grandmother used to like to talk about, especially in the starved months before she had died two years before, had long been replaced by the solemn celebration of the birth of a man named Jesus that all the missionaries said was what made all the things that had happened to Tlingit people in the seventy years before then so worthwhile. Jesus is the answer, they all insisted. Don't expect a reward here on earth, they reminded their Tlingit flock, you'll be rewarded in heaven after you die. It's too bad you've lost your fishing rights and your land and your language, they surely commiserated, but just think! You have the word of God! You'll walk on streets of gold! All you have to do, the missionaries instructed, along with the schoolteachers, judges, and doctors, is learn to speak and read God's own English while obeying all the new laws about what language your children now must speak, the laws about which people now get to

take your land for their own, the rules about which anthro-
pologists and explorers can now rob the graves of your ancestors, and the regulations about which tourists and which
shopkeepers can bring to town the whiskey they'll be happy
to trade for your family treasures. You must also remember
to obey God's holy commandments about always turning the
other cheek with regard to these blessed mysteries. Your suffering and poverty on earth will be rewarded by your joy and
riches in heaven.

Don't forget, though, the message unquestionably came,
that Native people must try to dress and talk like white people do, and a woman must never allow a man to touch her
outside the sanctity of holy matrimony. For almost as sinful
as doubt about the superiority of white people and all their
ways was the sinfulness of the body, made even worse by
experiencing any pleasure at bodily functions. Food must
never be enjoyed too much, it was understood, especially
primitive food like seal grease and fish eggs. Such primitive
enjoyment could lead to hell. Belching or passing wind from
any bodily orifice must never be done. Such uncivilized actions can lead to hell. Funny old stories about where fresh
water came from must never be cause for laughter. Those
stories can lead to hell. Ungodly fornication must never be
committed. No sexual congress could be undertaken until
the act had been duly consecrated by a white Man of God
and his signature flourished onto a special piece of paper.
After marriage, it was understood, women must never, never
seem to enjoy their wifely duty. If a woman took pleasure in
such a thing or if she seemed to enjoy any of the many other
sinful bodily acts, she'd be on her way to hell, and her life
would be hell here on earth before she was cast into the next

hell, which had been constructed by white people and their stern but loving God for the women who committed such ungodly acts.

My mother never spoke of these things, but the times and the territory made them all too clear. It was my mother's good fortune that her mother hadn't succumbed to the white man's newly delivered religion and had only sent her with her brothers and sisters to the white man's Christian church for Easter services and for Christmases, just in case there would be extra food to bring home or maybe a few presents for the unfortunate children of sinners. Even in those sporadic visits to Sunday school, though, my mother could not have helped but absorb the messages. Everyone understood what it meant to be unmarried and pregnant, and to be unmarried, pregnant, and unloved could only have been worse.

In the Ketchikan stop of our tour, I became melancholy and found myself thinking about my mother, seeing her on the streets she'd walked and in the window of the downstairs flat where she'd lived. She'd been younger then than I am now. She had had eight more years to live. Might that have been the reason for my melancholy there in Ketchikan? At my visit to Ketchikan, did I have eight more years to live? If so, I'll be seventy-seven years old when I die—a ripe number for someone who has lived a life like mine. If so, I will treat myself to another cup of coffee and love this life this view this moment. This life.

⚬ ‖ ⚬

Old Tom walks along the beach. He's feeling like a superstar these days. Though he might have been locked up for a day or two, it had been nothing like the drunk tank, and when he got to court, the charges were reduced and the judge let him go with time served. Old Tom supposes he could have turned it into an issue and insisted on having a trial, but he was never the political sort. He just wanted to get out of that place. So he took the deal, and now he walks along the beach a free man.

A free man, and a hero to some, it turns out.

Old Tom has always attended the gatherings of dance groups they hold every two years or so. Or at least he's always walked by the places where they're dancing. And certainly he's always stood along the curb as the dancers and drummers and singers along with their children and uncles and aunties and grandmas and grandpas parade down the street on their way to the hall where they pay fees to dance for their relatives and where their cousins pay fees to sell the handmade treasures and trinkets they arrange on the tables they rent from the hall and where everyone else pays fees to watch the dancers and to be excited and comforted by their songs and by their exhortations.

Before he sobered up, though, Old Tom never actually went inside the place, since until now he'd always thought the ten dollars it would take to see his relatives line up on a stage so they can sing invitation songs and mourning songs to an audience seated in a hall would be better spent on wine. But these days he's sober, so this time he paid his money for the green wristband that would gain him entrance for the day, and walked inside the building beyond the ticketsellers, where he became full of renewed outrage at the merchants who had money as their only concern. Full of impetuous zeal, he overturned their tables of cash boxes and trinkets, tore the plastic bracelet off his wrist, and called at the top of his voice for the fat cat directors of his own corporation to come among the people and show their own proofs of payment.

Guards rushed up. Police were called. At first they all thought Old Tom had finally fallen off the wagon. Before long he was brought before court, where his bored public defender saw another quick way to make quick money in another quick deal. The agreement was struck, and out the door Old Tom walked.

And so it came to pass that Old Tom walks to his button of a cove a free man, a freed man, a hero to some, and to others a superstar.

And now Old Tom walks again along the beach. Since that time he was proclaimed something of a hero, people sometimes want to come with him. Old Tom doesn't know how he feels about that. In one way, people following him to a place that was once only his to know might turn out to be uncomfortable, something he will wish he hadn't done. In another way, people following him to a place that was once only his to know can be nothing but a good thing. This little button of a cove wasn't meant to be hidden away from everyone. Old Tom decides that this place is for everyone who can find it, whether they stumble upon it on their own as he did, or whether they find it because someone has led them.

On this day, though, Old Tom wonders how to be a good host. Clearly the crowd of people who have assembled here on this bright fresh day are having a good time. Young men walk with their children, young mothers carry their babies alongside. Mabel and Lucille have brought the grandchildren so they can play. Patricia and Leonard help with the children and keep the fire going with driftwood collected by Alfred the Skiff Man. Even Jerry the White Man is laughing and calling jokes and long-time-no-see to others along the beach. The memory of Young Tom is running along the shore. The memory of Old Tom's father is telling stories. Everyone is here, even the ancestors. Everyone is here, even that old grandmother, the one who despite everything still loves and believes in her grandson. Even she is here. Everyone is watching the children. All the people are supporting and balancing one another. All the women are smiling. All the men feel strong.

When people feel thirsty, they press their faces against the cold snowmelt stream falling down the shining rocks. Children splash it on their faces and accept that this is what they are to do when they become thirsty. What are they to do when they become hungry?

Some of the crowd wonder if they should drive over to the fast food place and buy something for the children to eat. One or two of the mothers look to Old Tom for advice. Let everyone just sit down, Old Tom tells them. Let them sit on the logs and on the sand and on the grass. I have frybread here from last week. I have dryfish I've been saving for just such a day as this. There's enough for everyone, he assures them.

Old Tom tears generous pieces from frybread that has been stored in a greasy sack. There's more than enough to go around. Old Tom breaks dryfish into good-size pieces for everyone. Everyone is satisfied. Everyone becomes full. There's more than enough to go around.

There's still plenty left for all the ones who will come after.

❧ ‖ ❧

I allow myself to wonder at my father as a man whom a woman could love. But the picture in my mind can only promote him from the man who didn't love me, who didn't want to see me, to the man who existed because my mother always said she loved only him. On the day they met, on the day she allowed herself to wonder at the possibility of such a man, on that shining day, she must have wanted not to frown at this man, my father, this man of all men, this man who must have smiled at her in a way she found unfamiliar, this man who must have seemed to see her. No doubt she wanted to smile. There in the restaurant where she was paid to serve anyone who walked in the door with a demand, she must have subdued the racket of background clatter and the overpowering delicious smell of fried onions and the constant fear of underarm stain from the kitchen's heat and the heightened stress of the more-than-usual commotion and the piercing sting of hope for a man's attention and she must have managed to meet his dancing ghost-blue eyes and must have given him back her own brave smile.

I imagine my mother was aware that when she felt awkward she intensified her frown, so she must have called on the strength of will that had seen her through many trials but none so fearful as this. She probably astonished herself with a friendly, perhaps even saucy, reply. Taking a deep breath, she must have torn herself away from his dancing eyes and walked to the back of the house. She probably felt his gaze every step of the way. No doubt she heard and saw and felt nothing else.

The next time she blinked, the next time she breathed,

and every time she took a breath or blinked from that day forward, I know that she was somehow always back at his table. I'm sure that she would afterwards remember a Glenn Miller song playing on the jukebox, a song that later memory would trick her into hearing as "At Last" when she felt melancholy and as "St. Louis Blues March" when her memory focused on the image of herself walking, dancing, strutting, smiling, laughing, flirting. Jaunty. Happy. At the end of her life, when she couldn't dislodge her thoughts from the images of all the things that might have been, her memory served her no sound at all except the music of his voice when he whispered that he loved her.

⊹ ‖ ⊹

When I was about eight years old, living in the family house at the edge of the village with my mother, my grandmother, aunts, and uncles, along with their transit friends, my mother allowed me to adopt a red puppy. An Irish Setter. Long ears, burnished silk for hair.

In those 1950s days in territorial Alaska, we listened to the radio for news and entertainment. Sparkie and *No School Today* for Saturday morning company. The *Lone Ranger*. Local news that always ended with the words Good night and good flying. Suspense programs that featured creaking doors and echoes of ominous footsteps.

One spring morning, the radio played bird calls. That half-grown red setter paced faster and faster from the front room to the kitchen and back and back again and again, whining and whimpering, chasing unreachable sounds in the air.

Later on a summer afternoon, that red setter lay stretched out at the edge of the paved street that led cars away from the village dirt to the clean-looking houses perched on the hill above. She'd flopped into the relaxed pose she favored when she dreamt of birds she'd heard but never seen. One of the village kids asked me what was wrong with her. "She's dying," I joked, and I ran to her side to rouse her for play. She couldn't stand. She never got up. She died there.

A few years later, as I was walking to Zach Gordon's teenage club—where the Auke Kwaan building now sits, where in one of my last innocent, hopeful years I had attended fifth grade, where I had recently begun showing up to flirt and smoke and dance the jitterbug with Delphin and Tucker and white boys who drifted by, where I failed to learn the power of a tight red skirt—I was stopped by a friend. What are you doing here, he asked. Haven't you heard about Buzzy?

What's wrong, I joked. Is he dead?

My Uncle Buzz had lost his fight with alcohol. He died on a sidewalk in the cold rain.

That was the last time I joked about death.

The image of my grandmother dying alone on the road to Thane, the sight of my mother struggling to breathe, the mystery of my Uncle Skip, whose death was certain news after years of his rumored dying, the occasional I-wonder-what-ever-happened-to, the ever-growing, ever-present, ever-sharper who-will-be-there-for-me-when-it's-time-to-help-me-die—such thoughts spread themselves in the sunlight at the edge of my childhood memories. When I try to laugh, I hear calls coming from a place I can't see, a place I don't yet understand, while my years pace faster and faster and I chase unreachable sounds in the air.

My grandmother doesn't realize that she's old and I can't decide if I am young. Between the two of us there rests no hope at all. No matter that the men are out carousing, no matter that the men deny their children, no matter that all the women are fatherless. Songs in the night last longer than shadowed breaths. But we still have time to be frightened.

The women will carouse with half-strangled men and bring them home to sing in the night and bring them home to challenge the tide and bring them home to defend their shattered beds. The woman crying in the forest croons a lullaby, the child hiding in the night invents the rain.

The men carousing toward home will never arrive. Nothing covers us enough to avoid the dawn. I don't know how we survive this trauma. I don't know where we should start. I don't know which way to go. I don't know how it's done. I don't know who I can trust. I don't know when I will die.

But sometimes when I'm about to close my bedroom door behind me I think it could be the last time. As that other poet pointed out, I've lived through almost seventy anniversaries of the day I will die—and I feel regret and sorrow that someone, probably someone I love, will have to deal with this mess and I resolve to clean everything vacuum the carpet wash the clothes fold the laundry throw away what I don't wear anymore and never will. Toss out those crumpled scraps of forgotten brilliance dust the damn bookcase dust the damn TV just admit I'll never read most of those damn novels. Change the sheets even though that mattress is eighteen inches thick if it's a day. Freshen the bedspread carry those dead root-beer soldiers down to the recycle bin.

And then I close the door and by the time I'm halfway down the stairs I've forgotten that I will ever die at all.

＊ ‖ ＊

Raven teaches us to enjoy every thing that comes our way, to fill our bellies and empty our minds, to warm ourselves by the fire and cool ourselves with the taste of water, to doze into slumber when the dawn is about to break, to drift into sleep at the end of our years.

＊ ‖ ＊

I gather my owned things. I send a deer inviting you to help me push away my sorrow. When you agree, the time is arranged.

You arrive. I sing my cry song. You arrive, I sing my cry song. You arrive. I sing my cry song.

The song to end sorrow hasn't yet been written. The song to end my sorrow hasn't yet been sung. The song to end this sorrow warms my hands.

Remove the signs of your grief. Wash the sorrows from your face. It is time to sing a love song to my opposites. It is time to bring out my loved ones and show them to my guests. Their spirits reside in these owned things. Their spirits live in these owned things. Their names are carried on. I carry their names and burn good food for their robust meal so they will be warm and full and will know that I continue to carry them. I push away my sorrow. While they stand here with me, I stand in for them.

You are served plates full of my best food. Sit! Eat! Receive my thanks! At the time for laughter, I race bowls full of my best fruit for you to play and pretend to struggle. We can both use some laughter.

I speak and sing. You answer. I bring out my wealth. You answer. We reminisce. We remember. We laugh and push away our sorrow.

You are served plates full of our best food. Sit again! Eat again! Receive again my thanks! Laugh and sing and talk and receive this wealth. You wiped away my tears and I repay you. You carried my loved one to her grave and I repay you. You opened the ground for the ashes of my loved one. And I repay you with my songs and my food and my laughter and my wealth. I repay you with this fire and this light.

Out of a scrap of earth the image of a resolute cabin once emerged. But now its modest garden has been overgrown. Now the few windows through which a woman once took comfort from the sight of falling rain have dimmed and blurred and no longer allow light even on the brightest of days. The garden and the windows and the woman herself have fallen like leaves from a timeless forest.

More than leaves have fallen on this sodden scrap of earth. Life and memories and stories and happiness and friendship and regret and sorrow have fallen to their places and now enrich this steadfast scrap of earth. All good things have fallen to the ground: the drop of water from the leaf, the leaf itself, the cabin, the mother, the child. All the life that has come before us has fallen. All the life that will come after us will fall. We will all rejoin this scrap of earth and we will patiently wait. We will season ourselves in vigilant repose. We will listen for the lovesongs of those who tend the fires and we will await the inevitable dawn.

Inside an unnamed house not far from a cool dark stream, a spider waits. Outside, the raven calls.

ACKNOWLEDGMENTS

I SEND MY FIRST THANKS to editor extraordinaire Regan Huff, whose interest and encouragement brought this book into its existence. Gunalchéesh. I give heartfelt, continuing thanks to the Rasmuson Foundation, whose generosity allowed me to spend important time in the Djerassi Resident Artists Program in Woodside, California, where I assembled many threads into this woven work.

Great thanks to the Alaska Literary Awards program in the persons of Peggy Shumaker and Joe Usibelli, whose support of Alaska arts allowed me to return for a time to the waters of Southeast Alaska, the timeless comforting Inside Passage where so many find inspiration, and where I finalized the manuscript that became this work. Gunalchéesh.

Special thanks to friend and fellow writer Carrie Enge, always the first to read my work, and to Frank Soos and Nancy Lord for their encouragement. Gunalchéesh.

I offer recognition to those writers whom I have had the honor of meeting and who pave the way for all of us: Linda Hogan, Susan Power, Joan Kane, Ishmael Hope, Nora Dauenhauer, Simon Ortiz, and many others. Gunalchéesh.

ACKNOWLEDGMENTS

Finally, my loving thanks to Joshua and Robert; to Kiersten and Laihla; to Giovanna and Davis; to Andrew, Baby Josh, and Hunter; and to all those yet to come. You are my generations. Gunalchéesh.

ERNESTINE HAYES (Tlingit) is professor of English at the University of Alaska Southeast and the 2016–2018 Alaska State Writer Laureate.